Multimedia for Windows 95 Made Simple

Simon Collin

MADE SIMPLE
BOOKS

Made Simple
An imprint of Butterworth-Heinemann Ltd
Linacre House, Jordan Hill, Oxford OX2 8DP
A division of Reed Educational and Professional Publishing Ltd

ᴙ   A member of the Reed Elsevier plc group

OXFORD   BOSTON   JOHANNESBURG
MELBOURNE   NEW DELHI   SINGAPORE

First published 1997
©Simon Collin 1997

British Library Cataloguing in Publication Data
A catalogue record for this book is available from the British Library

ISBN 0 7506 3397 2

Typeset by P.K.McBride, Southampton

Archtype, Bash Casual, Cotswold and Gravity fonts from Advanced Graphics Ltd
Icons designed by Sarah Ward © 1994
Printed and bound in Great Britain by Scotprint, Musselburgh, Scotland

COMPUTING
MADE SIMPLE

ERBACK

WINDO
MADE SI

WORD
FOR WINDOWS 95
MADE SIMPLE

KEITH BRINDLEY

THE
INTER
FOR WINDO
MADE SIM

ACCESS
FOR WINDOWS 95
MADE SIMPLE

MOIRA STEPHEN

These books explain the basics o
software packages and computer
in a clear and simple manner, pro
just enough information to get st
For users who want an insight int
software packages and computers
without being overwhelmed by technical
terminology they are ideal.

- **Easy to Follow**
- **Task Based**
- **Jargon Free**
- **Easy Steps**
- **Practical**
- **Excellent Value**

ALL YOU NEED TO GET STARTED

NT (Version 4.0)
8   1997

ve
y
6   1997

Internet
gton
4   1997

Navigator
gton
2   1997

The Internet
gton
3   1997

net for Windows
nd Edition)
le
5 1   1997

net for Windows
d Edition)
le
6 X   1997

7 for Windows
le
8 6   1997

nt 97 For
s
Moira Stephen
0 7506 3799 4   1997

(version 2)
Moira Stephen
0 7506 2309 8   1995

P. K. McBride
0 7506 2836 7   1996

BESTSELLER
Internet for Windows 3.1
P. K. McBride
0 7506 2311 X   1995

Microsoft Networking
P. K. McBride
0 7506 2837 5   1996

NEW
Access 97 For Windows
Moira Stephen
0 7506 3800 1   1997

Pageplus for Windows 3.1 (Version 3)
Ian Sinclair
0 7506 2312 8   1995

Designing Internet Home Pages
Lilian Hobbs
0 7506 2941 X   1996

NEW
Word 97 For Windows
Keith Brindley
0 7506 3801 X   1997

BESTSELLER
Windows 95
4.0)
4   1996

NEW
Excel 97 For Windows
Stephen Morris
0 7506 3802 8   1997

Contents

Preface

Welcome to *Multimedia Made Simple*. Multimedia is the most exciting area of computing at the moment and it's also great fun to experiment with. This book explains everything you need to know to get started in multimedia using Windows 95.

This book covers how all the different parts work, how to use them and what to do with them. We also look at creating your own multimedia titles: from an interactive catalogue to simple sounds in a memo.

Multimedia software is all the rage: exciting games, animations, encyclopaedias, all available on CD-ROMs. This book shows you how to install commercial software, how to use it and how to tune your PC so that the software will really fly!

The complex hardware and software components are explained and we'll show you how to upgrade your PC to take advantage of multimedia.

Multimedia Made Simple was fun to write, and I hope it makes multimedia just as much fun for you to learn about.

1 Introducing multimedia

The jargon

Like all sections of computing, multimedia is packed with jargon. What's worse is that since the technology is still developing, the jargon changes with it. In this section are described the basic terms that go with multimedia and will help you get going with the rest of this book.

Multimedia

Multimedia is any software or presentation that combines different media: sound, video, images, and text. You can buy multimedia applications (for example, that describe with pictures, spoken commentary and video how the human body works or how computers work) or you can create your own presentations and applications.

The screenshot below is from Dorling Kindersley's 'How Things Work', an example of interactive multimedia at its best. The clearly labelled buttons at the top and left allow you to find information easily.

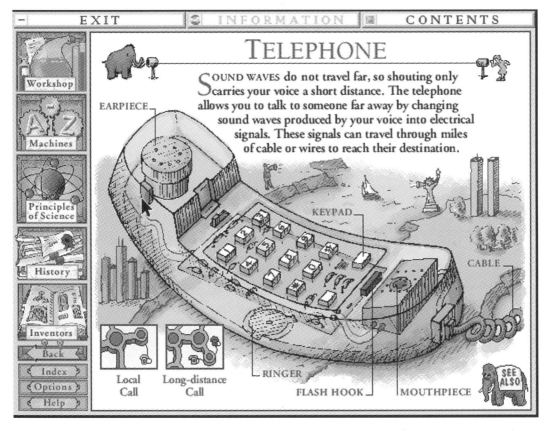

Hypertext

Multimedia applications often have hypertext links. A hypertext link is a special word, button or picture that, if you click on it, will move you to another page or display a piece of text. It's often used to show more detail about a particular topic. The special words with links to another page are normally described as *hot-words* or *hotlinks* and are displayed in a different colour. If you move the mouse pointer over a hotword, it changes shape to look like a hand .

Page

Multimedia applications are normally made up of pages. Each page is really a screen-full of information. If you are creating your own multimedia application, you can place text, buttons, images, sound or video clips on each page then link the pages together so that a user can move through the '*book*' (the name for a complete multimedia application with several pages).

Button

A button is a little icon on screen that normally starts something if you click on it. Simple buttons are just square outlines, others have shading to make them look three-dimensional. Buttons can start a video or sound clip or move to another page.

Sometimes plain text is clearer than any image.

Take note

There is a glossary of multimedia terms at the back of this book.

Some buttons carry text and images – there's no doubt what this button is for!

These buttons use similar symbols to those found on tape and video players.

Even if you had never met them before, you would soon work out which ones were Play, Rewind and Fast Forward.

Video clip

A video clip is sequence of images that are displayed rapidly to give the impression of movement. To give smooth motion, your PC needs to display over 25 frames every second - each frame is a separate image, so even a short video clip takes up a huge amount of space on your disk. If you want to record video clips from a video camera or television, you'll need special hardware to plug into your PC. If you want to play back a video sequence, you don't need any special hardware.

Take note

To capture some types of data from outside your PC you will need special hardware: a scanner for images, a video camera for video and a micro-phone for sounds.

Still from a video clip

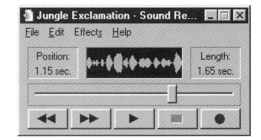

You can edit sounds easier if you can see them (more in Chapter 3)

Sound

Your PC can play simple beeps through its speaker or, by adding a sound card, you can record and play back stereo CD-quality sound or control electronic drum machines and synthesizers.

Images

With a high-resolution colour monitor you can display life-like images and edit them using paint software (see Chapter 6).

What is multimedia?

❑ In this book you will see how these technologies work, how to control them and how, with the tools built into Windows 95, to use them in your own applications to make memos more exciting, presentations more eye-catching or create your own interactive software.

Interactive multimedia lets you move around the pages of the electronic book by clicking on buttons, images and text. Each page can contain images, sound, video, text and buttons.

Multimedia software is created on packages such as IconAuthor. With this, you can draw together images, sounds and text, and control the way they interact with each other – and with the user.

There is a lot of confusion about what exactly is multimedia. It is a presentation, game or application that combines different media. Your computer can use video clips, sound recordings, images, animation and text, and can control external devices such as a video recorder, video disc player, CD-ROM drive, synthesizer and video camera.

If the program plays a sequence of sound, video and images, this is *multimedia*. If the program lets the user control the sequence by selecting different options, it is called *interactive multimedia*.

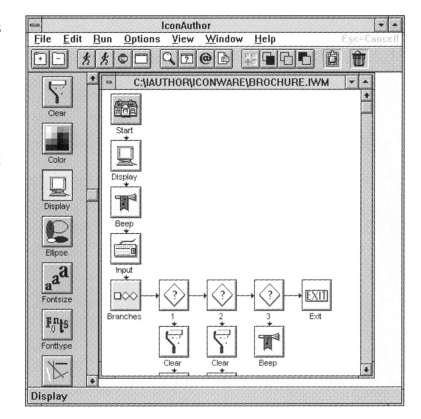

Developing your own multimedia

Multimedia is one of the most creative areas of computing because you don't need to be an programmer to create an application. Once you have mastered recording sounds, editing images and blending these together, you will be able to tackle simple authoring tools that let any non-programmer create stunning results.

The screenshot below is taken from Music Station, with it you can write, edit and mix musical compositions.

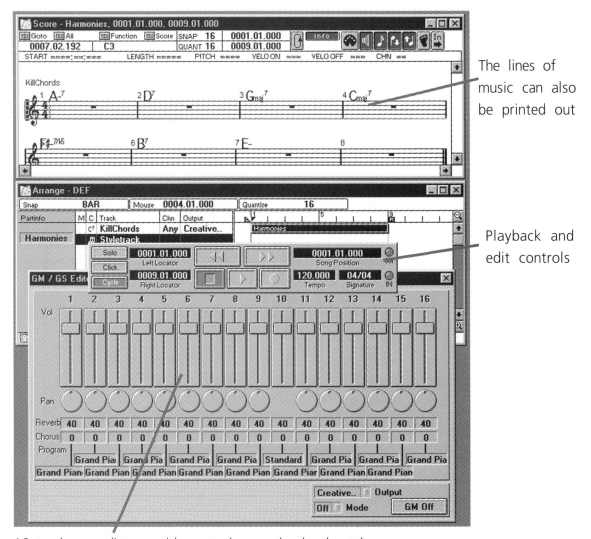

The lines of music can also be printed out

Playback and edit controls

16 track recording – with control over the level, style – and the instrumental voice – of them all..

Multimedia and Windows

The multimedia revolution hit the PC with the release of Microsoft Windows 3.1, and is now even easier to use with Windows 95. This has all the tools you need to get started with multimedia. Windows 95 lets you access any CD-ROM drive, move files to your hard disk and play back sound, video or animation files.

Windows 95 also has utilities that let you record sounds onto your hard disk then edit them or add special effects. It lets you play back video clips, paint images and control external equipment including synthesizers, video discs and music CDs.

Sound Recorder

This utility controls the sound card installed in your multimedia PC. Through Sound Recorder, you can record sounds, edit them, add effects then play them back in stereo, CD-quality.

CD Player

This program lets you play standard music CDs in your PC CD-ROM drive. You can listen to them through speakers, or through headphones plugged into the front of the drive.

Media Player

This can control a video disc or audio CD, and can play back multimedia files including video clips, sound recordings, animation sequences or MIDI music files.

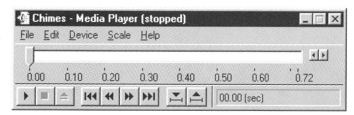

Windows Explorer

Once you have installed a CD-ROM drive in your PC, you can access it through the Explorer program. It's also useful if you are installing commercial software from a CD-ROM or if you want to copy clip-art or other files from a CD-ROM onto your hard disk.

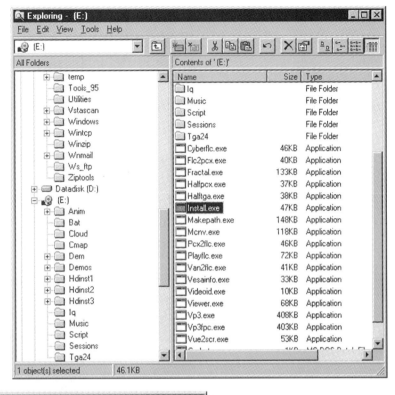

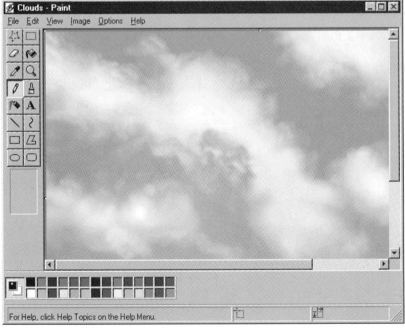

Paint

This utility lets you create your own images. You can edit existing images, or paint and draw images to use as a background to an application, or design your own icons or buttons.

2 Multimedia hardware

The equipment

Before you can start to use the multimedia features of Windows, or run a multimedia application, you must have the correct hardware on your PC. If you bought a multimedia-ready PC then you should have everything you need – but it is still worth reading the next few pages to make sure that you understand what each new piece of hardware does.

To get going with multimedia, your PC should have:

Sound card

This plugs into an expansion slot in your PC and converts digital data from the PC into sound - it also lets you record sounds onto your hard disk.

CD-ROM drive

This should be next on your shopping list. The drive is the device into which you place the CD-ROM disc; it also needs a special controller card that fits into an expansion slot in your PC. You can use the CD-ROM drive to access commercial applications on CD-ROM or to play normal audio CDs. To save your own files onto a CD-ROM, you need a special, more expensive drive that records data onto special CDs.

If you are a keen photographer, you can use your CD-ROM drive to access PhotoCD discs. When you send your film in to be developed, you can ask the laboratory to make a PhotoCD (a special type of CD-ROM) on which are stored high-resolution colour scans of your photographs.

Take note

More adventurous users might want to eventually add a scanner (page 19) to capture images or a video camera (page 18) and capture card to record video sequences.

The ROM in CD-ROM stands for Read Only Memory, and distinguishes them from audio CDs. You also get ROM chips, which have programs permanently built into them – as opposed to RAM (Random Access Memory) chips which only hold data and programs while the PC is running.

Memory

Make sure that your PC has enough main memory (RAM). You will need a minimum of 8Mb to run Windows 95 and 16Mb is recommended. If you are likely to edit large images or video clips you will need more RAM, or your PC will seem to crawl. (See page 22 to find out how to check your RAM.)

Graphics adapter

Last on the list is the graphics adapter, which you will need to display high-resolution images in colour. This is either built into the main electronics of your PC or is supplied as a card that fits into an expansion slot. The current standard is S-VGA, which can display pictures with a resolution of 800 x 600 pixels, or even 1024 x 768 pixels, in thousands of colours.; if you have an older VGA adapter you should be able to run most multimedia software – but check before you buy it.

Tip

If you are working on a PC that belongs to your company, don't add any new hardware or software until you have checked with the IT manager or PC support staff.

The MPC specification

To make it easier for anyone trying to buy a suitable PC for multimedia use, the MPC (Multimedia Personal Computer) specifications define the minimum requirements.

If a PC is MPC compliant it will have an official sticker that proves this and will let you run most multimedia titles. An advancement of the MPC standard is called MPC-2; this lets you display higher quality images and record clearer sound.

If the PC you want to buy doesn't have an MPC sticker, it does not mean that it cannot run multimedia software. Most new PCs now come with enough resources built in to run multimedia, and many manufacturers sell upgrades cheaply.

The CD-ROM drive

A CD-ROM disc is a small plastic-coated disc that holds information as tiny holes in a central metal layer. It looks and works just like a normal audio CD. A laser beam is used to 'read' the holes in the disc as it spins in the drive.

To spin the disc and control the laser you need a CD-ROM drive and to interface the CD-ROM drive to your PC you need a controller card. Some sound cards have a CD-ROM controller built-in, otherwise you will need a special card called a SCSI card (see page 14 on how to install a card).

CD-ROM drives can either be fitted inside your PC in one of the free $5\,^1/_4$-inch drive bays in the front panel or can be fitted externally. External drives have their own case and power supply and are useful if you need to share a drive between PCs – but you will still need a controller card in each PC.

At the front of all CD-ROM drives is an access slot for the disc. There are two ways of inserting the disc, which vary according to the drive. Some manufacturers use a caddy: you fit the disc inside the plastic caddy (which looks rather like a CD case) and then slide the whole lot inside the drive. Other drives use a tray - like an audio CD player; a motorised tray slides out from the drive and you place the disc on top and push it back into place.

SCSI stands for Small Computer Standard Interface and can be used for connecting CD-ROM drives, scanners and other devices to a PC.

Free drive bay for CD-ROM drive

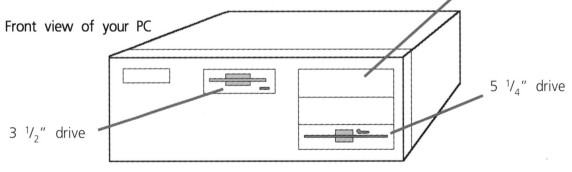

Front view of your PC

3 $^1/_2$" drive

5 $^1/_4$" drive

Music while you work

Front view of CD-ROM drive

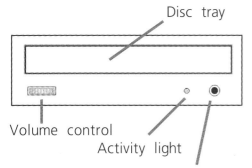

Disc tray

Volume control

Activity light

Headphone socket

Below the disc access slot is a socket for a pair of headphones, together with a volume control. Almost all CD-ROM drives can play audio CDs which you can listen to by plugging in a pair of headphones. You control the play, stop and fast-forward functions from the Media Player or CD Player utilities in Windows.

Media Player will play your audio CDs.

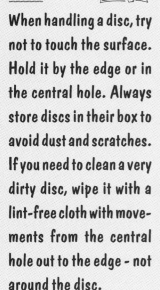

Tip

When handling a disc, try not to touch the surface. Hold it by the edge or in the central hole. Always store discs in their box to avoid dust and scratches. If you need to clean a very dirty disc, wipe it with a lint-free cloth with movements from the central hole out to the edge - not around the disc.

Buying decisions

The speed of a disc drive is measured by its access time: a fast drive has an access time of less than 250msec. This describes how fast data can be located on the disc. A second measure describes how fast the data is then transferred to the PC: a quad-speed drive transfers data at four times the speed of an older drive by spinning the disc four-times faster. If you're playing video titles the speed of the drive will effect the quality of the video playback.

In order to use a PhotoCD disc, which can store photographic images (see page 72), you will need to make sure that your CD-ROM drive is multi-session compatible. If it is a CD-ROM/XA drive then it can read XA discs that hold both video and audio data.

13

The sound card

A sound card fits inside your PC into an expansion slot and converts digital data from the PC into sound waves which you can listen to by plugging a pair of speakers or headphones into the sound card. The card can also record any sound from a microphone by converting it into data which can be stored on your hard disk.

Recording sound

The card works by a process called sampling. A sound wave is an analogue signal – a constantly changing signal. As a computer can only handle numerical data, i.e. digital sounds, it has to convert the sound into a number form.

The card does this by looking at the level of the voice signal repeatedly (actually several thousand times every second) and noting the level of the signal at that time. This converts the signal into a stream of numbers that describe its height as it varies with time. It's these numbers that are be stored on disk.

Playing sound

Playing back a sound normally works in exactly the reverse to recording: the computer passes a stream of numbers to the card which turns these into an analogue signal by changing the level according to the number, amplifies the signal and plays this through the speakers.

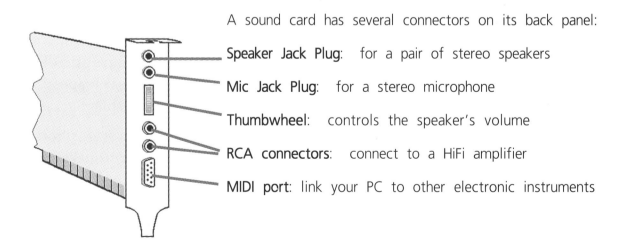

A sound card has several connectors on its back panel:

Speaker Jack Plug: for a pair of stereo speakers

Mic Jack Plug: for a stereo microphone

Thumbwheel: controls the speaker's volume

RCA connectors: connect to a HiFi amplifier

MIDI port: link your PC to other electronic instruments

Volume

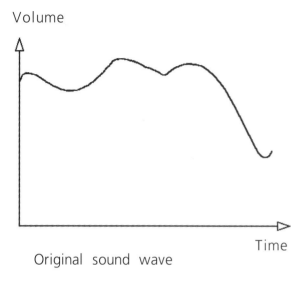

Original sound wave

Time

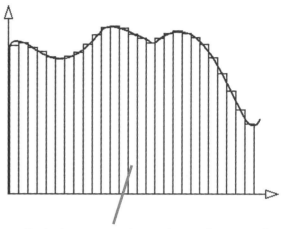

Each is a 'sample', where the sound card measures the level of the signal

Sample rate

To record fine detail in the signal, the card has to be able to sample very fast. This can generate a huge amount of data, so you have a trade-off between the amount of data and the accuracy of the recording. For normal voice recordings, you need a card that can sample at 11.01KHz (11,000 times per second), for high-quality audio you should use 22.05KHz and for studio-quality sound 44.1KHz is a must.

Sample size

The sample rate is only part of the story: the second factor that effects quality is the size of the sample word. For example, many sound cards use an 8-bit sample word; each sample is stored within 8 bits and so can be one of 256 different numbers or levels. For a more accurate representation of a signal you need to distinguish between finer levels in the samples; a 16-bit sample can differentiate between 64,000 levels but takes twice as much space on the disk as an 8-bit sample.

MIDI

Sound cards almost always have a MIDI port. This is a high-speed serial port used to connect your PC to electronic musical instruments, such as a keyboard or drum machine. Windows includes utilities that let you record the notes played on a drum machine and play them back later.

A synthesizer

For more sophisticated musical effects, you can control external electronic instruments using the MIDI interface on your sound card. You can plug in up to 32 instruments such as a keyboard, drum machine, or synthesizer.

The MIDI port transmits musical notes to each instrument, or record notes from each instrument to the PC. It can also select special effects: for example, the controlling software on your PC could select a tin-drum and then send a series of notes, change to a piano effect and send the same series of notes. The software can also record notes played on an instrument, so the PC can act as a type of digital tape recorder.

Other features

Your sound card might also contain a waveform synthesizer chip. This is another way of creating sounds using a set of pre-recorded noises stored in a chip on the card. The music software controls how the noises are mixed together to create new sounds.

MIDI stands for Musical Instrument Digital Interface and is a standard for connecting electronic instruments and compatible computers.

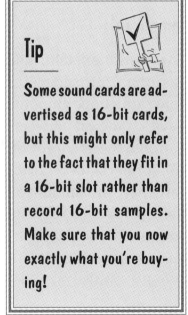

Tip

Some sound cards are advertised as 16-bit cards, but this might only refer to the fact that they fit in a 16-bit slot rather than record 16-bit samples. Make sure that you now exactly what you're buying!

The graphics adapter (page 11) on your PC controls the individual pixels – the tiny points on a screen – that make up a character or image. To display colours, the brightness of three colours (red, green and blue) pixels is varied and, to your eye, they combine to look like a colour.

Almost all new PCs come fitted with a graphics card that can support the VGA standard. This allows images of up to 640 x 480 pixels to be displayed in up to 64,000 colours. Watch out – many commercial multimedia applications now require higher quality graphics than VGA, normally the S-VGA standard that increases the resolution to 800 x 600 pixels. Many PCs are now supplied with a graphics card that can display 1024 x 768 pixels, for even clearer pictures.

In order to display the output from a graphics adapter you need a monitor that is capable of supporting the correct resolution. If you are upgrading your graphics adapter, make sure that the monitor can support the resolution of the new card.

Graphics adapter RAM

The graphics adapter has its own memory area on the card that is used to store the image that's being displayed. Many cards allow you to increase the amount of RAM fitted to the graphics adapter – and this will immediately increase the number of colours or the resolution that the card can display.

Buying tips

The quality of a monitor is described by its dot-pitch – a measure of how fine the individual pixels: the smaller this number, the sharper the image.

A local bus graphics adapter is a good choice if you intend to do a lot of image or video editing. A local bus moves data faster, and is fitted to high-performance PCs.

Tip

When you buy a new PC, it may have been set up to use a standard, low, resolution. For clearer graphics, you can change the settings easily under Windows (see page 135).

Image capture

Video cameras

If you are feeling adventurous – and rich – you can expand your PC to allow it to capture video clips from a video camera, TV or VCR. The video capture card typically stores around 25 frames of images every second. Since each frame is a complete colour image, storing video takes up a vast amount of disk space: for example, 10 seconds of video could easily take up 2 – 3Mb of disk space. (Hard discs are getting cheaper. You can now pick up a 1 Gigabyte drive for under £200.)

Video playback

You do not need special hardware in order to play back video clips on your PC. Video clips are stored in a compressed format with an AVI file extension. The Windows Media Player utility will let you play back video clips.

Take note

In Windows, the standard way of storing video clips is the AVI (Audio-Visual Interleaved) format.

These files contain both sound and video, and their filenames have an .AVI extension.

Windows Media Player is a simple but effective video playback system; here the video sequence is displayed in a small window below the control panel.

A scanner

A scanner is very useful if you want to import logos, images or graphics into your PC. For simple work, a hand-held scanner provides a cheap way to import images. For more accurate work, or for better definition, a flat-bed scanner is recommended.

A scanner works rather like a photocopier: it shines a light onto the paper to be scanned and a light-sensitive head passes over the image, detecting the light reflected from the image. This is then converted into a form which can be displayed in a paint or drawing package.

A hand-held scanner normally comes with its own interface card that fits into an expansion slot of your PC. A flat-bed scanner normally connects to a SCSI controller card; if you have a CD-ROM drive you probably already have a SCSI controller into which you can plug the scanner.

Take note

Scanners convert a picture into a series of tiny dots; the number of dots depends upon the resolution of the scanner. For best results, get a scanner that scans images at twice the resolution of your printer.

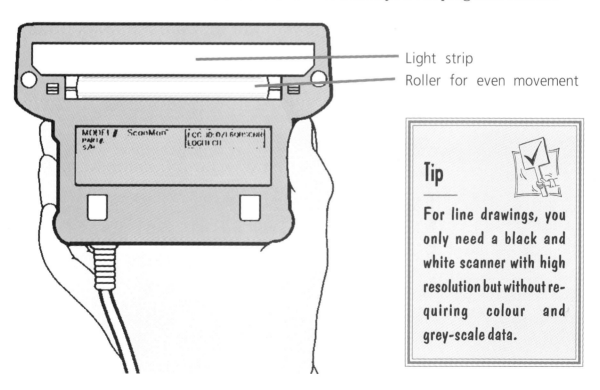

Light strip

Roller for even movement

Tip

For line drawings, you only need a black and white scanner with high resolution but without requiring colour and grey-scale data.

Summary

❏ **Multimedia** is the use of a combination of sound, text, video and graphics.

❏ Windows includes many **utilities** to control multi-media devices and play back sound or video clips.

❏ For a **good setup**, your PC needs at least 8Mb of RAM, a CD-ROM player, sound card and a colour S-VGA monitor.

❏ The **higher the quality** of sound recorded, the **more disk space** it needs.

❏ More **advanced systems** can control video discs, video cameras and synthesizers.

❏ If you want to import pictures and photographs into your system, you will need a **scanner**.

3 Upgrading your PC

Installing new hardware

If you want to use commercial multimedia titles, you will need a CD-ROM drive. (See page 12.)

For almost all multimedia applications, you'll need a sound card. (See page 14.)

Your PC will need at least 8Mb of RAM. If you plan to use video or do a lot of image editing, you should increase this to at least 16Mb.

To see this, double-click on the System icon in the Control Panel and select the Performance tab from the Properties display.

System

Tip

If you have a multimedia-ready PC, then you can skip this chapter and get straight onto experimenting with multimedia.

The memory fitted to this PC is shown in the first line of the Performance tab of the System Properties panel.

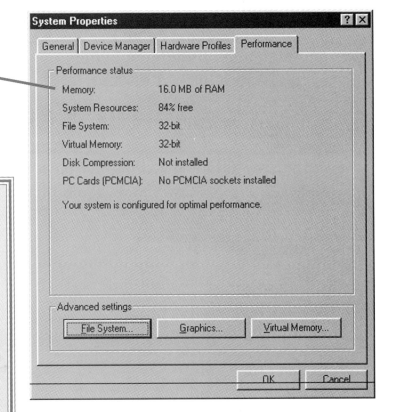

System Properties

General | Device Manager | Hardware Profiles | Performance

Performance status

Memory:	16.0 MB of RAM
System Resources:	84% free
File System:	32-bit
Virtual Memory:	32-bit
Disk Compression:	Not installed
PC Cards (PCMCIA):	No PCMCIA sockets installed

Your system is configured for optimal performance.

Advanced settings

File System... | Graphics... | Virtual Memory...

OK | Cancel

Take note

Windows 95 does a very good job of configuring itself, and most new hardware is designed to take full advantage of this. In most cases, adding a new device involves little more than plugging in the hardware and running its installation software.

Basic steps

Installing a card

1 Switch off your PC, unplug the mains lead and open the case.

2 Find the row of expansion slots, remove the metal cover plate from the back of a free slot.

3 Press the new card firmly into the slot, with the metal plate with connectors to microphone or speaker facing out.

4 Secure the metal plate onto the PC's chassis using the screw you took out in step 2.

5 Put the case back on, plug in the mains and switch on the PC.

6 If it doesn't work, read about interrupts in its manual, and use the Device Manager tab of the System Properties panel to edit the setting.

Installing a new card into your PC is one of the basic ways of expanding its functions. You might need to fit a sound card or, if you're adding a CD-ROM drive, you may need a special controller card. Cards fit inside your PC into long connectors, called a expansion slots. Most PCs have five or six slots, but some might already be used by a graphics adapter card or hard disk controller.

Installing the driver software

For the PC to control the card, it needs special driver software to translate the data from the card into a form that the PC can understand. Newer 'Plug and Play' cards set themselves up and configure Windows automatically. Older cards need you to configure them and to install the driver. The software will be on a disk with your new card. Each type has a different installation procedure, so read your card's manual carefully and follow its instructions.

The PC communicates with a card in an expansion slot using a special signal called an interrupt. Each card needs to be allocated its own interrupt number, or you'll confuse the PC. The installation software normally sets this up correctly, but if you do have problems, read the card's manual for advice on setting interrupts.

Take note

When you switch on your PC, it will carry out basic tests on itself, if there's a problem it will beep several times. Switch it off and check that you fitted the card correctly.

Configuring Windows

The next step before you can use your new card is to configure Windows and tell it about the new hardware and the driver software.

Windows 95 is very good at working out automatically how to use a new piece of hardware.

To set up your new card, you'll need to use a Wizard – a utility that helps you to configure the card.

③ Double click the icon

Add New
Hardware

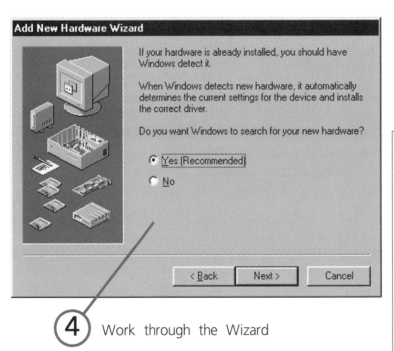

Add New Hardware Wizard

If your hardware is already installed, you should have Windows detect it.

When Windows detects new hardware, it automatically determines the current settings for the device and installs the correct driver.

Do you want Windows to search for your new hardware?

⊙ Yes (Recommended)
○ No

< Back   Next >   Cancel

④ Work through the Wizard

Basic steps

1 Read the manual for specific instructions.

2 From the **Start** menu, select **Settings** then **Control Panel** icon.

3 Double-click the **Add New Hardware** icon.

4 Follow the Wizard through its steps – let Windows try to work out how to configure the hardware.

5 If there is a problem, re-check the manual and follow its methods.

Tip

Adding and configuring new hardware works for sound cards, CD-ROM drives, graphics adapters, mice, joysticks and any other peripherals. To configure the particular device, you'll need to set it up as described on the next page.

Basic steps

Configuring new hardware

1 In the **Control Panel**, double click on the **Multimedia** icon.

2 Select the tab for your new device.

3 Configure the settings for the card – e.g. a sound card will have volume control.

Now that Windows has been set up to recognise the new hardware, you can configure your PC so that Windows and the hardware work correctly.

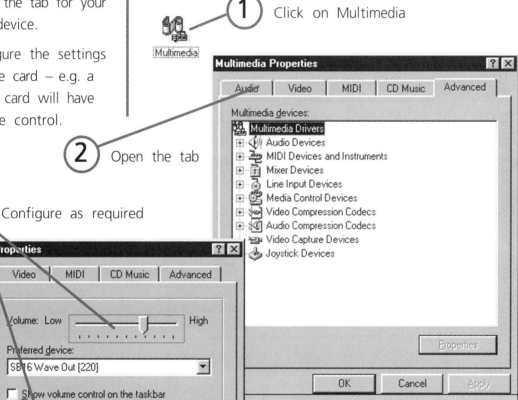

(1) Click on Multimedia

(2) Open the tab

(3) Configure as required

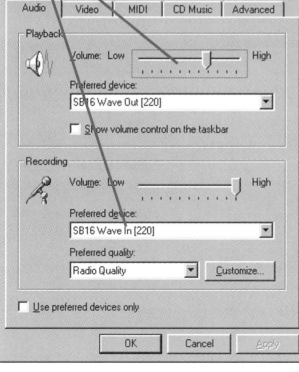

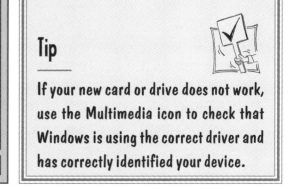

Tip

If your new card or drive does not work, use the Multimedia icon to check that Windows is using the correct driver and has correctly identified your device.

Installing more RAM

RAM is the memory that your PC uses to store programs and data you are using. It's much faster than disk storage, but more expensive and will only store data when the PC is switched on. For serious multimedia work in Windows 95 you should have 16Mb.

RAM is fitted in the form of electronic 'chips', these are mounted in sets of 8 or 9 onto a tiny card called a SIMM (Single In-line Memory Module).

SIMM cards fit into SIMM sockets in your PC. These are little sockets that are around 3-4 inches long. Your PC probably has four or eight sockets, and you will probably find that several are already full.

1 Switch off your PC, unplug the mains lead and open the case.

2 Find the row of SIMM cards fitted and the empty SIMM sockets.

3 Press the new SIMM card firmly into the expansion connector.

4 Put the case back on, plug in the mains and switch on the PC.

PCs running Windows 95 detect the additional memory automatically.

Memory chips

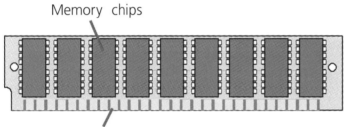

Gold connectors that fit into SIMM socket

When buying SIMMs, you will be asked what size and speed you want. Check in your PC's manual to see what type of SIMM card it requires and the speed that it supports.

Take note

SIMM cards are very sensitive to static, so hold the cards by the edges and try not to touch the black squares (the RAM chips) on the cards.

Take note

You cannot mix SIMMs. If you already have, say, two 4Mb SIMMs, you can only add more 4Mb SIMMs. You may have to remove the old SIMMs and install all new ones to be able to increase memory as much as you want.

Basic steps

Installing a CD-ROM drive

1 Unplug your PC, and open the case.

2 Remove the panel from an empty drive bay.

3 Slide the CD-ROM drive into the bay and screw it into position.

4 Connect a spare power lead – there will be several.

❑ **Controller cards**

5 Fit the card into a free slot – see page 23.

6 Connect its ribbon cable to the drive.

❑ **IDE CD-ROM drives**

7 Plug a connector from the hard drive's ribbon onto the CD-ROM drive – with the red stripe at the No 1 pin.

8 Set the hard drive to make it the *master* – see its manual for details.

9 Connect the CD-ROM drive's audio cables to the sound card.

Fitting a CD-ROM is not very difficult, but there are several steps to the process and you must follow them carefully.

All CD-ROM drives are the same size as a 5$\frac{1}{4}$-inch floppy disk drive. If you want to fit one into the front of your PC, you'll need to make sure that there's a free slot on your PC's fascia. Alternatively, you can use an external drive linked to your PC by a cable. The only difference is that an external drive has its own power supply.

Some CD-ROM drives are controlled by a special card that fits into an expansion slot in your PC. Normally this interface between the controller card and the drive uses the SCSI standard, but some sound cards have their own interface to a CD-ROM. The newest standard is called SCSI-2 and is faster than the older SCSI standard, but will still work with older equipment.

Some drives are controlled by the same IDE interface than contols the hard drive. These should be connected to a spare connector on the ribbon cable that runs from the main board to the hard drive.

When the CD-ROM drive is in place, follow the steps in *Setting up Windows*, to configure it into your system.

Take note

Make sure that you have the correct type of controller card for the CD-ROM drive. If you buy an upgrade kit, everything will be compatible, otherwise try to stick to SCSI-compatible equipment as this will work together and is easier to upgrade.

Summary

❑ **Check what your PC has fitted** and make a list of what it needs.

❑ To **install a card**, switch off your PC, open the case and plug in the card.

❑ Before the card will work properly, you need to install the **driver software**.

❑ You may occasionally have to set the **interrupts** to make a card work with your system.

❑ If you are installing more **RAM**, you don't need to configure Windows.

❑ **Installing a CD-ROM** is quite straightforward, as each cable has one – and only one – matching socket.

❑ Some CD-ROM drives are **controlled by special cards**, others work with the PC's standard **IDE controller**.

❑ After adding any new peripheral to your system, you should use the **Add new hardware** routine in the Control Panel.

28

4 Sound

Sound Recorder

Once you have installed your sound card (see page 14) you are ready to starting recording and playing back sounds. Windows includes a utility called Sound Recorder that allows you to record a sound then save it in a standard file format called a WAV file. Once you have recorded a sound, you can use Sound Recorder to play it back, add special effects or edit it. Over the next few pages you will see how to use Sound Recorder and how to use the WAV sound file in other programs.

To start off, make sure that you have plugged in the microphone into the **Mic** socket of the sound card and a pair of speakers into the **Speaker** socket. Turn the thumbwheel volume control on the back of the sound card to around its half-way point – you can adjust this later.

The Sound Recorder utility is on the Accessories – Multimedia menu. If you don't have this menu, or you cannot find the Sound Recorder icon there, check with your computer manager if you work in a company or install the utility from the Windows setup CD-ROM.

Take note

The Sound Recorder uses WAV files that contain sampled sound signals. A MIDI file (see Chapter 5) contains notes rather than actual sound samples.

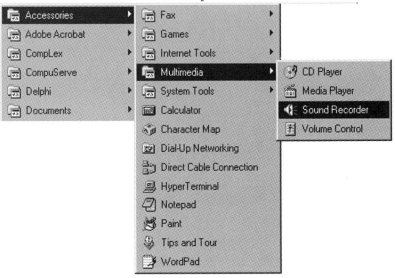

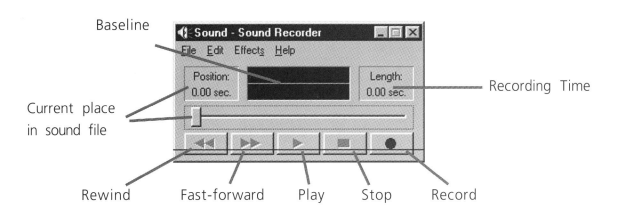

Baseline

Recording Time

Current place in sound file

Rewind   Fast-forward   Play   Stop   Record

When you start Sound Recorder you will see a control panel that looks very similar to an audio tape recorder. The buttons work in much the same way, allowing you to play a sound recording, rewind to the beginning, fast-forward to the end or stop during playback.

In the central part of the panel is a thin green line running horizontally across the playback window. This line is called the **baseline**. It shows the shape of the sound signal as it is being recorded or played back.

To the left of the baseline, the Position panel tells you the current place in the file. The slider shows the same information graphically.

To the right is an indicator that tells you how long the recording is. Sound Recorder normally has a maximum recording capacity of 50 seconds – but if you record for this long the resulting file will be nearly 1 Mb!

Tip

Try to record for no more than around 20 seconds, or the WAV file on your disk will become very big.

31

Recording a sound

Basic steps

1 Start **Sound Recorder** by double clicking on its icon.

2 Hold the microphone between 20 – 30 cms from your mouth.

3 Click on 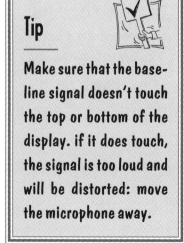 the Record button to start recording.

4 Speak into the microphone.

5 When you have finished, click on 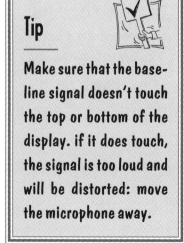 the Stop button.

6 Use **File–Save** to save your sound as a file.

Before you start, make sure that you have the microphone plugged into the sound card and switched on (if it has a switch).

To start recording, point to the record button and click the left-hand mouse button. Speak into the microphone, but don't hold it too close to your mouth, or you will record a lot of hissing. As you speak, you'll see a waveform representation of your voice on the baseline and the current length of the recording.

Once you want to stop recording, click on the Stop button. The recorded sound is stored in memory, but it has not yet been saved permanently to disk. Use the File–Save menu option to save the sound as a WAV format file.

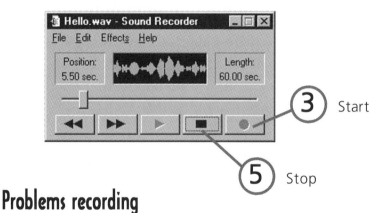

(3) Start

(5) Stop

Problems recording

If the baseline doesn't show a signal as you speak, make sure that you correctly selected the Record button. If there's still no signal, you might have to set up the sound card input level – some cards set it to zero by default! Check your card's manual to see if there is a mixer or setup utility that lets you set the input level of the microphone.

Tip

Make sure that the baseline signal doesn't touch the top or bottom of the display. if it does touch, the signal is too loud and will be distorted: move the microphone away.

Basic steps

1 Select the **File–Open** menu option.

2 Highlight the WAV file you saved earlier, or look in the Windows directory for samples then click **OK** to open the file.

3 Click the Play button to start.

4 Click the Stop button to stop, then the rewind button to move back to the start of the sound sample.

Once you have recorded and saved a sound as a WAV file you can play it back using Sound Recorder. The window title bar will show the name of the sound file and the green baseline will show the shape of the sound wave.

To play, click on the Play button. The slider moves to show which part of the sound is being played – you can drag this to move to a new part. To the left of the baseline is an indicator with the current position.

To stop playing the sound, select the Stop button. This doesn't move back to the start of the sample, so either click Play again to continue or click the Fast Forward or Rrewind buttons to move to the end or start of the sound.

Adjusting the volume

If you want to adjust the volume of the sound, you can either adjust the amplification of the sound card with its thumbwheel, use the Windows 95 Volume Control utility or change the sound sample itself (see page 37).

Tip

Click to the right of the marker on the scroll bar to move forward in the sample by one second, or to the left of the marker to move back by one second.

Take note

If you want to record from your Hi-Fi system, you will get better quality sound if you connect the Hi-Fi amplifier output directly to the sound card using the two line input sockets on the back of the sound card.

You must have copyright permission if you want to make commercial use of anyone else's sounds!

Editing sounds

Recording a voice or a sound does not always result in the perfect sound sample. You might pause before speaking, or cough in the middle! Sound Recorder includes simple editing functions that let you cut out sections of a sound sample that you don't want.

There are two cutting functions: one cuts any sound before the current point and the second cuts the sound after the current point. With these, you can trim a sound sample to remove, say, a cough at the start or a pause at the end. By combining them, you can cut out sounds in the middle of your sample.

The editing functions work in relation to the current point in the sample. This exactly in the middle of the playback window, and although there's no line or mark, with a bit or practice you will get to know exactly where it lies.

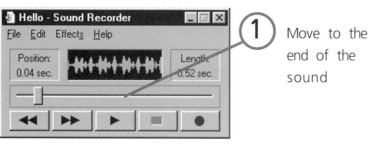

Move to the end of the sound

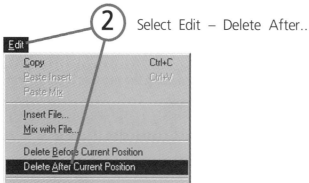

Select Edit – Delete After..

❑ **To cut off the end**

1 Move the marker in the scroll bar to get to the end of the sound you want. The end of the wave should be in the centre of the baseline.

2 Select the **Edit – Delete After Current Position** menu option.

3 A message box will ask you to confirm that you want to delete this section of the sample, click **OK** if you are sure.

4 Press the Play button to check that the sample now ends at the correct point. If okay, save the file with the **File–Save** menu option. If you want to go back to the original sound, choose the **File–Revert** menu option.

Basic steps

1 Open the first file and use **Delete Before** and **Delete After** to trim it down to the section you want. Save it!

2 Repeat with the second file. Save it – just in case of later errors.

3 Move to the start of the second sound file.

4 Use **Edit–Insert File**.

5 Reopen the first file. It will be inserted at the current position.

6 Save the new sound.

Running sounds together

To add two sounds so that they run on from each other, use the Sound Recorder's **Insert File** function. This will insert an existing sound sample at the chosen point in your existing sound. For example, if you have one sound sample with you saying 'hello' and another saying 'world' you could combine them to say 'hello world'.

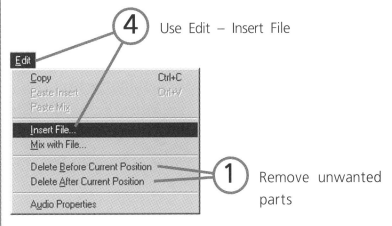

④ Use Edit – Insert File

① Remove unwanted parts

⑤ Select the file

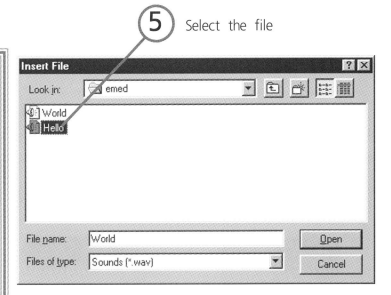

Take note

If you need to remove a section from the middle of a file, trim it down to the wanted start and end, saving each separately – you'll have to reopen the file to get the second half. It's long-winded, but the only way to do it without special editing software

Mixing sounds together

A good of enhancing any sound sample is to mix it with another. For example, if you want to add applause to a speech, or a background mood-music to an announcement, you need to mix two sounds together. Sound Recorder lets you combine two sound files so that they play simultaneously.

Record your speech or announcement and save this as one WAV file. Now record your background effects or applause and save this as a second WAV file. The Mix function in Sound Recorder will combine the two.

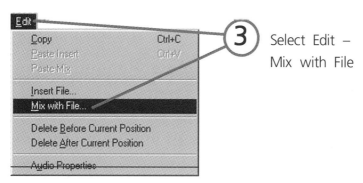

Select Edit – Mix with File

Volume levels

When you mix two sounds together, the signals are added together. This means that the overall level of the finished sound could reach the limits of your sound card and so start to distort. If your two sounds are too loud, you'll have to reduce their volume using the Edit/Reduce Volume menu option.

High volume – with distortion at the limits

Low volume – clearer signal

Basic steps

1 Record your speech and save it as 'sound1.wav'.

2 Record your applause and save it as 'sound2.wav' – this is the file currently open.

3 Select the **Edit – Mix** menu option.

4 Highlight the file 'sound1.wav' and click **OK**.

5 The result is a mix of sound1 and sound2. Select Play to hear your speech with applause.

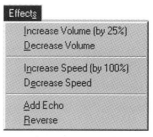

The Volume controls are on the **Effects** menu.

36

Basic steps

❑ To change the volume

1 Select **File – Open** and highlight your sound WAV file, click **OK**.

2 Choose the **Effects – Increase Volume** option. Repeat if a further increase is wanted.

3 Play back the sound – it will be 25% louder.

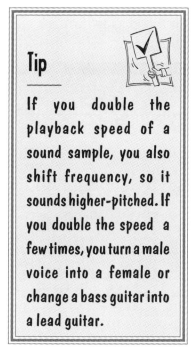

Tip

If you double the playback speed of a sound sample, you also shift frequency, so it sounds higher-pitched. If you double the speed a few times, you turn a male voice into a female or change a bass guitar into a lead guitar.

Special effects

Sound Recorder includes several special effects that help enhance your sounds.

● **Volume control** changes the sound wave, magnifying or reducing the level, and so the volume.

● Change the **speed** at which the sound is played back – see the Tip.

● **Echo** gives greater depth to speech and makes it sound more natural.

● **Reverse** simply plays the sound backwards!

All the effects work on the entire sound sample: you cannot choose to increase the volume of just one section.

Volume Control

Windows 95 has a Volume Control utility that will change the volume from the sound card. You can set different volume levels for each source of sound. If you are recording from a CD, for example, it is a good idea to turn the Microphone off, to avoid unwanted sounds.

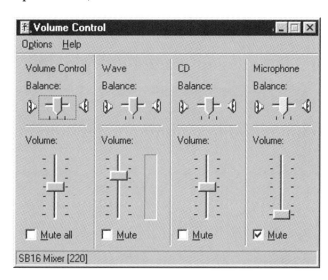

37

Sound editing software

Windows 95 Sound Recorder is sufficient to get you started on simple editing. If you want to change the pitch (the frequency) of a sound, or adjust the different frequencies within a sound sample then you will need to use a commercial sound editing program, such as **WaveWorks**.

1 Start WaveWorks and load the sound file using **File – Open**.

❏ **Cutting out a section**

2 Point to the start of the section, hold down the mouse button and drag to the end of the section. Markers show the start and end.

3 Choose the **Edit –Cut** menu option to delete this marked section.

① Open the file

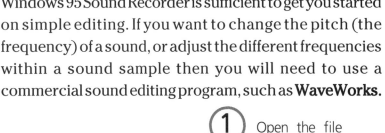

② Click and drag to mark the section

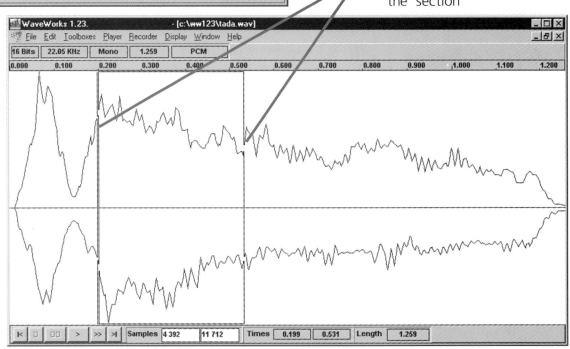

4 Use the **Toolbox** dialog boxes to edit the sound. **Preview** the effect before clicking the **Apply** button.

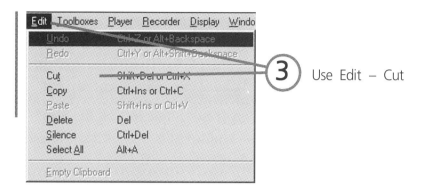

Use Edit – Cut

④ Edit the sounds

Change the frequency of the sound to get rid of any hiss or rumble (very high and low frequency sounds that distort music or speech)

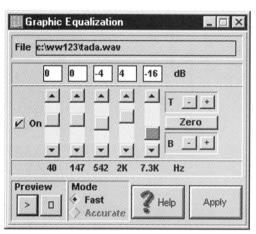

WaveWorks lets you fade-in or fade-out a sound so that it gradually gets louder or slowly fades away over a period of time

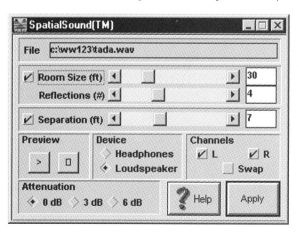

You can add depth to the sound to make it appear that it was recorded in a large hall.

39

Playing audio CDs

If you want to work with background music, Windows lets you play normal audio CDs in your CD-ROM drive. The CD Player utility has similar controls to a Hi-Fi CD player, and plays back via speakers, connected to the sound card.

Check if you have CD Player installed. It is on the **Start – Programs – Accessories – Multimedia** menu. If it is not, use these steps to install the software.

1 Open the **Control Panel** and double-click **Add/ Remove Programs**.

Add/Remove Programs

2 Open the **Windows Setup** tab.

3 Select **Multimedia** and click **Details...**

4 Check the **CD Player** box and click **OK**. Windows will install the software. (You might need the installation CD-ROM.)

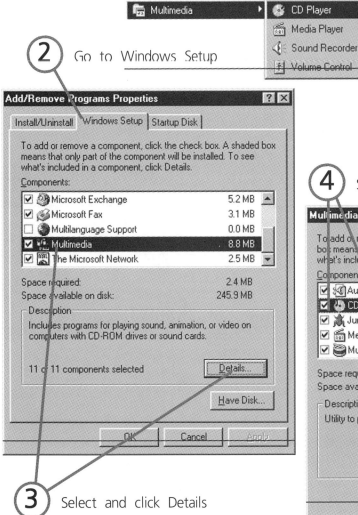

Select and click Details

Select CD Player and click OK

Basic steps

1 Insert the audio CD into the drive.

2 CD Player will run and start to play the first track. If it does not run automatically, run it from the **Accessories – Multimedia** menu.

3 Maximize CD Player.

4 To change the track order, select **Disc – Edit Play List**.

5 **Remove** tracks from the Play list then **Add** them back in the required order.

Controlling the audio CD

CD Player lets you set up the order in which tracks are played–you can even save this information, together with the name of the artist.

Lastly, you can record sections of the CD music using Sound Recorder–but you must have copyright permission to do this.

③ Maximize CD Player

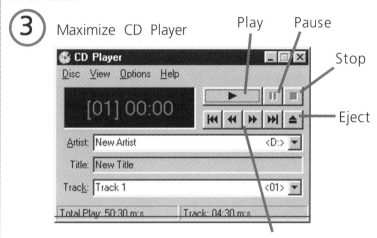

Play   Pause

Stop

Eject

Fast forward and rewind

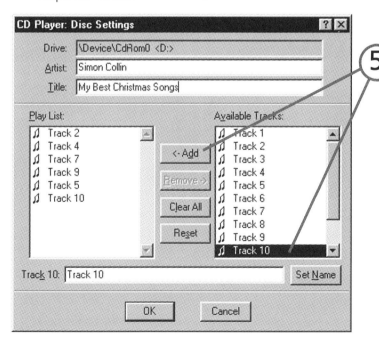

⑤ Add tracks in the order of play

Tip

You can open the Volume Control panel from the View menu.

41

Recording from a CD

Windows 95 lets you record the sounds from a CD onto your hard disk. You can do this using a combination of the CD Player and the Sound Recorder. To make sure that the procedure works correctly, you will also need to use the Volume Control utility to change the strength of the signal from the audio CD into the Sound Recorder.

The sounds or music that you record from an audio CD are stored on disk as a WAV file. You can then edit these sounds, attach them to an event in Windows (see 'Hooking sounds', page 44) or use the sound in a multimedia presentation.

1 Start the **CD Player**.

2 You will need to boost the CD audio level and cut the level of other sound sources: Select the **View – Volume Control** command.

3 Move the CD slider to its maximum and click on the **Mute** checkbox for the microphone.

4 Click on the **Options –Properties** in the **Volume Control** panel and select **Recording**.

(1) Start CD Player

(2) Select View – Volume Control

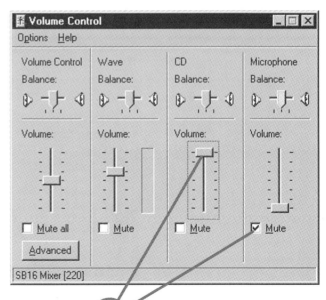

(3) Maximise the CD level and Mute the microphone

5 De-select the checkbox below each input except for the CD.

6 Start the **Sound Recorder**.

7 Move to the desired track with the Audio CD Player and click on the **Record** button on the Sound Recorder.

8 Save the sound as a WAV file.

④ Open the Properties dialog and select the Recording controls

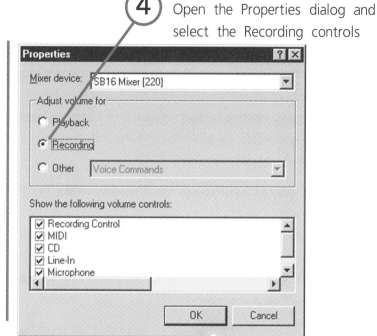

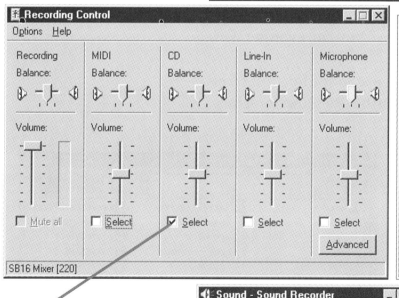

⑤ Turn off everything except the CD

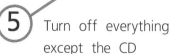

⑦ Start to record

Hooking sounds

With your PC equipped with a sound card, it's hard to resist not configuring Windows to take advantage of all the new sounds that you can capture and play back. Windows has half-a-dozen sounds that it uses if there's an error (normally a bell), or a fanfare (when it starts) or scales (when you quit Windows).

Each of these events is called a *hook*. You can assign any sound to these hooks – and there are plenty of them. For example, the bell soon gets irritating if you make a lot of mistakes; Microsoft Word sounds the bell if you try and scroll past the last line in the document. Some people might prefer a spoken warning.

The same when you start Windows – why not set it up so that your PC says 'Hello' to you and 'Goodbye' or 'thanks' when you shut down Windows? You can even get Windows to chime on the hour.

To create your own recording, use Sound Recorder (see page 32) and save the WAV file in the \Windows directory.

page 32

Tip

Windows includes about a dozen hooks, but some other applications can add their own.

There are a few WAV files already in Windows, to start you off. These are all assigned to hooks.

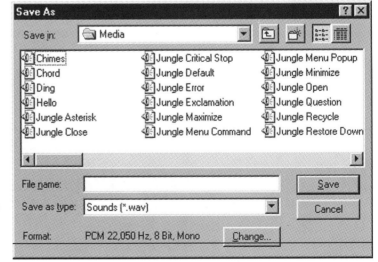

The Jungle sound files are from a Microsoft Plus! theme.

44

Basic steps

1 Open the **Control Panel** and double-click on the **Sounds** icon.

2 Select an **Event** from the list.

3 Select a **Sound** from the drop-down list.

4 Click the **Play** button to preview it.

(2) Select an Event

(1) Double click on Sounds

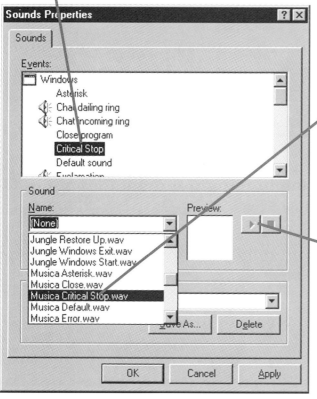

(3) Link it to a sound file

(4) Listen to the Preview

45

Karaoke

If you have always wanted to be a pop star, you can use your computer to help you practise by turning it into a multimedia karaoke machine, which lets you record the music from an audio CD and your voice from a microphone.

The process of recording from two sources relies on the Volume Control utility which allows you select multiple sound sources to record. We will use the CD Player to control the audio CD and the Sound Recorder to record the music from the CD and your voice from a microphone plugged into the sound card.

Basic steps

1 Start the **CD Player**.

2 Select the **View – Volume Control** command.

3 Move the **CD** and **Microphone** sliders to the maximum settings.

4 Select **Options – Properties** and select to view the **Recording** volumes and sources.

5 Select the **CD** and the **Microphone** and de-select the rest.

① Start CD Player

② Select View – Volume Control

③ Set the microphone and CD to maximum

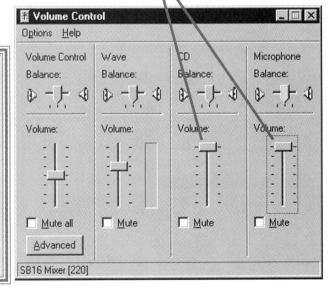

Tip

This is not just for fun, it is also a good way to record a commentary to a multimedia title with background music or special effects. Your local CD shop should have special effect CDs, with sounds of doors creaking, footsteps and more!

6 Start the **Sound Recorder**.

7 Use the CD Player to play to the correct track on the CD. At the same time, click the Record button on the Sound Recorder and sing or speak as the music plays. Save the sound as a WAV file.

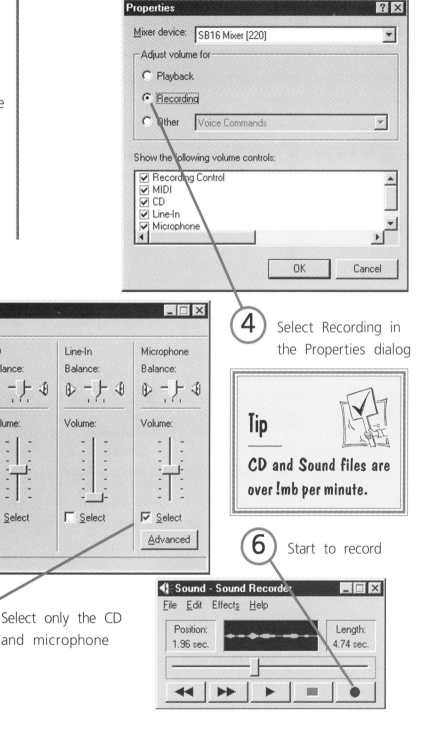

Select Recording in the Properties dialog

Tip

CD and Sound files are over !mb per minute.

Start to record

Select only the CD and microphone

Summary

❑ You can **record sounds** on your PC using a sound card to convert the signal into a digital form. The Sound Recorder utility is used to record sound samples which are stored in a WAV file format.

❑ The Sound Recorder can also be used to **play back** sound samples, edit them and add special effects.

❑ The **volume** of sound samples can be adjusted either using the thumbwheel on the sound card or through software.

❑ You can record sounds, special effects and music from an audio CD onto your hard disk using the CD Player and Sound Recorder.

❑ To play **audio CDs**, you need to install the correct driver then you can control your CD-ROM drive using the CD Player utility.

❑ You can record your voice as your sing along or add background music to a speech using a microphone and the CD Player.

❑ Add interest to your Windows configuration by **hooking your own sounds to events** within Windows.

❑ Reduce the levels of the sound sources that you do not want to record, just in case they interfere with your finished sounds.

5 Midi

MIDI

The MIDI (Musical Instrument Digital Interface) standard arose from synthesisers. It coveres the way that music is stored, and the physical and electrical connections between electronic instruments.

Files are stored as notes and isntrument names, not as digital recordings of sound wave (which WAV files are). As a result, they are far smaller. Half an hour of complex music stored as a MIDI file would probably be less than 1Mb – as a WAV file, the same music would take nearly 1Gb! If you want to create more complex musical effects, or play several different instruments at the same time, you need to learn about MIDI.

❑ Most sound cards have a MIDI synthesizer built in. An *FM synthesizer* creates sounds by varying the frequency of a basic note – it's simple and cheap but not as good as a *wave-form synthesizer*. This has short recordings of 'real' instruments that are played back.

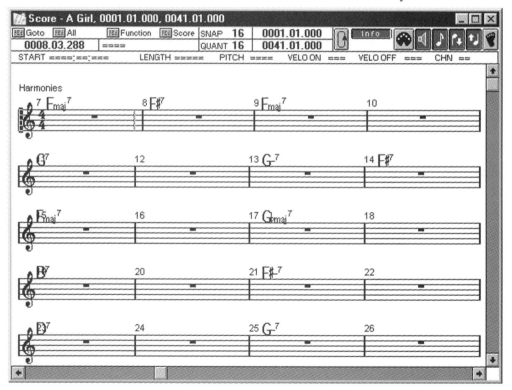

This MIDI sequencer software will record notes played on a synthesizer and display them – or you can write music directly onto the screen.

❑ To play a tune on a MIDI synthesizer you tell it the notes to play and the instrument to use. Each instrument 'sound' is described by information called a *patch* which defines what a piano, violin or drum sound like.

MIDI is normally used to control external electronic instruments, such as a keyboard or drum machine. These can be linked to a PC through the 9-pin D-connector at the back of a sound card. This is the MIDI interface and it works like a high-speed serial interface (it actually transmits the data at 32.5Kbps).

You will need a MIDI cable from your PC to the round connectors used by instruments: you can link several instruments together, in a daisy-chain fashion, and each can be controlled separately.

Windows' MIDI Mapper lets you assign each MIDI channel to a different instrument.

The **first 128 instrument sounds** in a synthesizer are usually always the same – until you change them! This means that if you want to use an oboe, you select channel 68

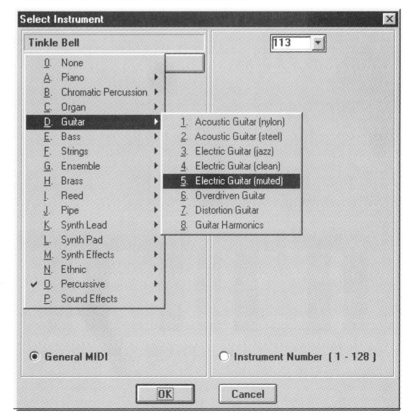

How to use MIDI

Windows comes with the Media Player (opposite) to play MIDI files, and MIDI Mapper to set the channels for a sound card sequencer, but nothing for composing using MIDI.

To create a tune you will need software called a sequencer – your sound card may well have come with one. This lets you write musical notes and assign them to different instruments: remember, MIDI can play several different instruments at the same time! You can create separate tracks for each instrument and compose the notes on that track, then play the tracks back together.

The sequencer should also have a mixer to let you change the volume of each track or instrument as it is being played.

❑ As you can see, MIDI is far more flexible and powerful than a basic sound card. It takes extra software and a lot of time to understand all its functions, but it's worth while if you want to create great music.

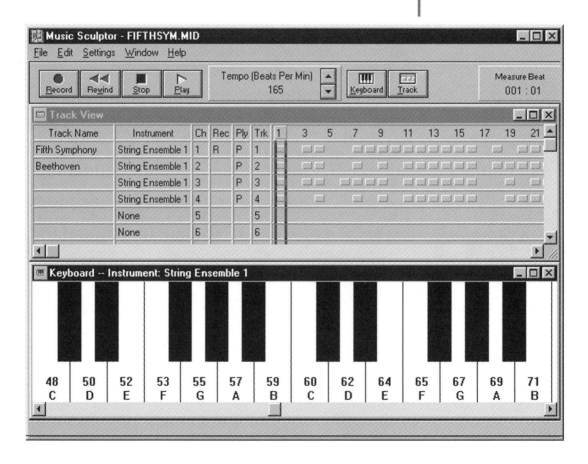

Basic steps

Playing MIDI

1 Run **Media Player**.

2 Use the **File – Open** menu option to find and open your MIDI file – it will have a *mid* or *rmi* extension.

3 Click ▶ the **Play** button.

MIDI notes and instructions are stored in files with a MID extension. MIDI files – created with a sequencer or pre-written samples – can be played with the Media Player.

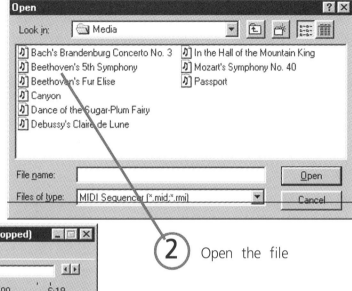

③ Click Play

② Open the file

Musical Notes

The MIDI information that is played back by Media Player consists of musical notes. Some MIDI software lets you view the normal musical notation or the full MIDI data.

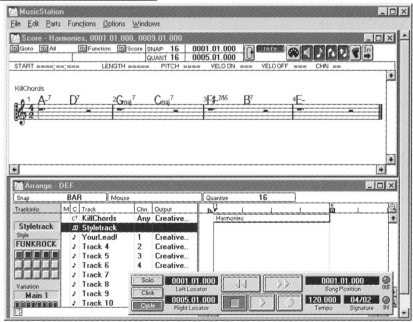

Connecting MIDI devices

If you have an external electronic instrument with a MIDI interface, you can plug it into the MIDI port on your sound card and control it from the sequencer.

You will need to buy a MIDI cable for your sound card. This plugs into the connector on the back of the card and feeds into two leads with round connectors. External instruments normally have two, sometimes three, MIDI sockets. These are labeled 'in', 'out' and 'thru'. You can connect up to 32 instruments together in a daisy-chain fashion and control them all from the sequencer software that's running on your PC.

Plug the cable from your PC into the 'in' socket of the first instrument, then a second cable from this from the 'thru' socket to the 'in' socket of the second instrument. This should lead back to the second MIDI lead on your PC.

Recording from MIDI

You can use your PC not only as a sequencer, but also as a recorder to record the notes played on other MIDI instruments. For example, if you can play the piano, you could set up your sequencer to record the notes generated by the electronic piano. Once you have recorded the notes you can play them back through any other instrument!

The control panel of many MIDI sequencers will display the speed at which you are playing notes and it is recording, and you can make a 'click' to help you keep time.

Advanced MIDI software

MIDI is the standard that's used by thousands of professional musicians. With a computer, a fully-featured sequencer and a suitable keyboard, you can have as much power as a professional recording studio sitting on your desk.

Advanced MIDI sequencer software can look daunting, but it's quite straightforward to use. There is normally an area where you can write the musical notes, and a mixing desk to vary the volume of the different instruments in the final work.

Tip

If you want **MIDI** music for your multimedia presentations, look out for the free files on magazine **CD-ROMs**. There is also plenty on the Internet – and some of this is copyright-free!

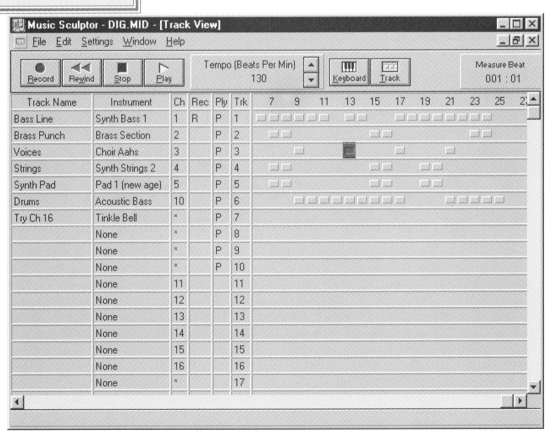

Track Name	Instrument	Ch	Rec	Ply	Trk	7	9	11	13	15	17	19	21	23	25	2
Bass Line	Synth Bass 1	1	R	P	1											
Brass Punch	Brass Section	2		P	2											
Voices	Choir Aahs	3		P	3											
Strings	Synth Strings 2	4		P	4											
Synth Pad	Pad 1 (new age)	5		P	5											
Drums	Acoustic Bass	10		P	6											
Try Ch 16	Tinkle Bell	x		P	7											
	None	x		P	8											
	None	x		P	9											
	None	x		P	10											
	None	11			11											
	None	12			12											
	None	13			13											
	None	14			14											
	None	15			15											
	None	16			16											
	None	x			17											

Music Sculptor - DIG.MID - [Track View]

File Edit Settings Window Help

Record Rewind Stop Play Tempo (Beats Per Min) 130 Keyboard Track Measure Beat 001 : 01

Summary

❑ MIDI is a high-speed serial link that can connect your PC to **external electronic instruments**.

❑ MIDI stores **notes and commands** to control instruments, rather than sound waves.

❑ Windows comes with software to play back files with MIDI notes, but you need **sequencer software** to create your own tunes.

❑ MIDI allows you to play many **different instruments** at the same time – to create your own orchestra!

❑ MIDI is the most flexible and powerful method of producing **musical effects**.

❑ With a PC, sound card, sequencer software – and preferably a keyboard – you have the basis of a professional music studio.

6 Images and graphics

Graphics

The way to make any multimedia presentation really stand out is with sparkling graphics. Windows' own Paint program lets you create simple, effective images, and is good enough for backgrounds, titles or simple animation. If you have a scanner, you can use Paint to edit the scanned images, adding special effects or cropping the picture to the size you want.

Paint can save bitmap graphic images in two of the most popular file formats: BMP and PCX. You can import images created with Paintbrush into just about any authoring program, presentation software or even your Windows wordprocessor application.

A bitmapped graphic in Paint. Later on, you'll see how to edit the image and add more towers to the church! Paint can read DIB, GIF and JPG as well as PCX and BMP files.

File formats

Graphics can be stored in many file formats, of which the most popular are TIFF, BMP and PCX. Each of these stores images in a slightly different way. The most important difference is in the type of image. There are two types:

- **Vector graphics** describe shapes using lines and curves. The image is stored as a set of co-ordinates, which are scaled up or down when you change the size of the image.

- **Bitmap images** are made up of pixels, tiny dots of coloured light. Magnifying the image increases the size of each pixel, giving a jagged edge to lines.

Below: a vector graphic in Micrografix Designer. The shapes are drawn with line 'vectors' and these remain as sharp even if you zoom in close.

Colours

Each pixel in a colour bitmap image can be painted a different colour. You'll often see paint programs described with the number of colours they can use. An image in Paint can only use 28 different colours, but you can choose those 28 from a palette with millions of colours.

The more colours you want to use, the more bits have to be used to describe each pixel and so the image file becomes bigger.

Paint allows you to save files in four levels of colour:

- Monochrome (Black and white), using 1 bit per pixel;

- 16 colours, using four bits per pixel;

- 256 colours, using 8 bits per pixel;

- 24-bit, giving a palette of 16.7 million colours.

High-quality, full-colour images take up a lot of disk space! If space is a problem, reducing from 24-bit colour to 256 colours will cut the file size to a third.

When you use a lot of images in a multimedia book, the book soon starts to grow in size, too. That's one of the reasons why so many colourful multimedia titles are sold on CD-ROM - nothing else can store as much data.

Resolution

As well as different colours, images are displayed in different resolutions (the number of pixels in each unit area). A VGA monitor has a maximum resolution of 640 x 480 pixels, regardless of the size of the screen. An S-VGA monitor should be set to either 800 x 600 or 1024 x 768 pixels, to make images look sharper and better defined.

Take note

Any computer image is better than a television, which has surprisingly poor quality - but because of the movement, your eyes don't notice the resolution (until you press freeze-frame on your video player).

Basic steps

Paint tools

❑ **To define a colour**

1 Double click with the right mouse button on the palette colour you want to change.

2 To open the panel click

> Define Custom Colors >>

A panel with the entire colour spectrum appear.

3 Choose a colour by clicking on the spectrum.

4 Click **OK**.

To start Paint, open the **Start – Programs – Accessories** menu and select **Paint**.

At the left of the screen is the toolbox, with a panel of options below (this varies with the selected tool). Along the bottom of the screen is the palette of available colours. The main blank area of the screen is your canvas.

To select colours, move to the palette and click once with the left button to set the ink colour, or with the right to set the colour of the background – this is important in filled shapes, when using the eraser and when starting a new image.

If you are using clip art or scanned images, they may need to be re-sized. You can set the size of the canvas (with the **Image – Attributes** command), but you cannot resize an existing image in Paint: to do this you need a more sophisticated paint program. (See page 66.)

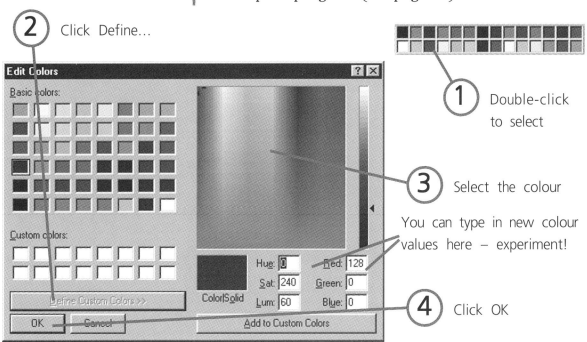

② Click Define...

① Double-click to select

③ Select the colour

You can type in new colour values here – experiment!

④ Click OK

Edit Colors

Basic colors:

Custom colors:

Hue: 0   Red: 128
Sat: 240   Green: 0
Color|Solid   Lum: 60   Blue: 0

Define Custom Colors >>

OK   Cancel   Add to Custom Colors

Editing images

You will probably find Paint most useful to retouch or edit existing images that you have scanned in or taken from a clip art source. Paint includes tools to duplicate an area, delete sections and paint one pixel at a time.

When your image has one rose, why not create a bunch of roses? If a background has one mountain, give it three. You can do this – without the joins showing – by using the copy and paste commands of Paint. First, define the area you want to copy, copy it to the Clipboard (an area of memory that can temporarily store images, sound or text) and paste it in where you want.

□ **To duplicate part of an image**

1 Click on 🔲 the free-hand selector tool at the top of the toolbar.

2 Move the pointer to one edge of the image to be duplicated, hold down the right button and trace around it.

① Use the freehand selector

③ Copy it

② Trace the outline

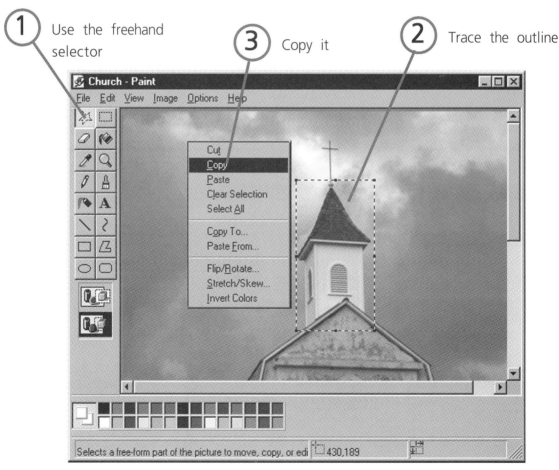

62

3 Release the right mouse button and select **Copy** to copy the selected area.

4 Select **Edit–Paste**. A duplicate image will appear at the top left.

5 Drag the new image into position.

④ Edit–Paste to get a duplicate

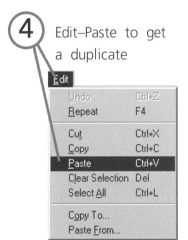

Edit	
Undo	Ctrl+Z
Repeat	F4
Cut	Ctrl+X
Copy	Ctrl+C
Paste	Ctrl+V
Clear Selection	Del
Select All	Ctrl+L
Copy To...	
Paste From...	

Take note

You can copy part of an image from one picture to another. Copy from the first picture, then open the second file and paste the image into it.

⑤ Move into place

Moving images

To move an area within an image, define the area with the freehand selector, and drag it to its new position. You don't have to cut or paste it.

Retouching images

Often when you scan in an image, you may need to edit it to get rid of a background that's distracting or little speckles that ruin the image. Here's how to edit the image at a fine, pixel-by-pixel level.

1 Select the **View–Zoom – Large Size** option.

2 Use the scroll bars to move to the area you want to edit.

3 Select colours from the palette for the ink (left button) and the background (right button).

(1) Zoom – Large Size to start

(6) Back to Normal

You can also Zoom in using the magnifying glass

(4) Click to change colour

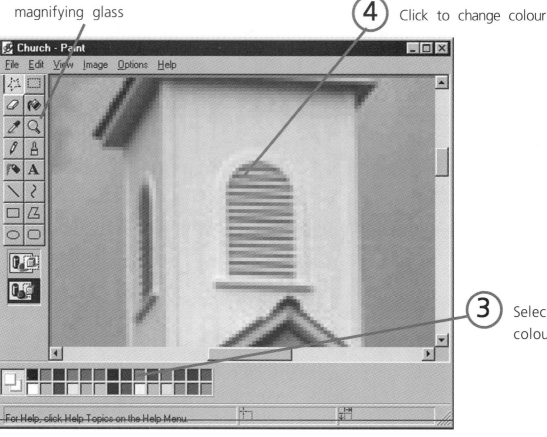

(3) Select colours

4 Move to the pixel you want to edit and click once with the left button to set it to the ink colour and once with the right button to set it to the background colour.

5 Repeat as necessary, using the scroll bars to move over the image.

6 Select the **View–Zoom – Normal Size** menu option to see the whole image.

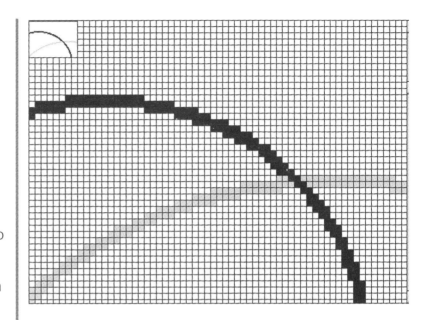

Dots of a lighter shade will smooth a jagged line

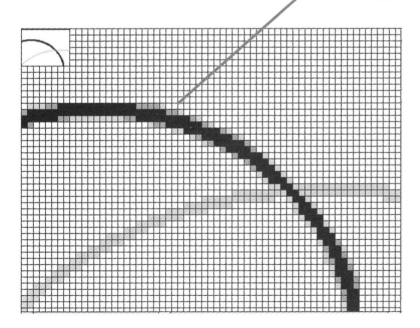

Tip

If you want to smooth out a line or curve so that it appears less jagged, add a lighter shade of the colour in the 'jags' and your eye will make it smoother.

Other graphics programs

There are two big advantages of Paint: first, it's free and second it's easy to use. If you want to create more complex graphics or special effects, for your multimedia work, you should really consider buying more advanced graphics software.

There are special software packages designed for different graphics jobs:

- editing full-colour photographic-quality images;
- designing complex three-dimensional models;
- drawing accurate graphics or landscapes;
- creating icons or special pointers.

Make sure you have the right tools for the job!

Many multimedia authoring packages include drawing utilities. Asymetrix ToolBook includes an icon and cursor editor, shown here, that lets you design your own icons and cursor shapes to use in your application.

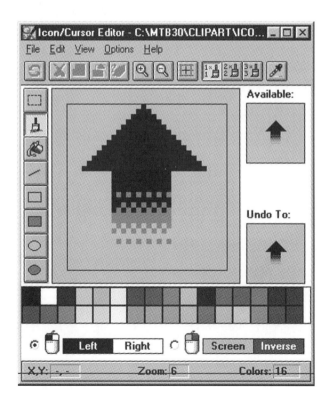

One advanced program that is excellent value for money is called Paint Shop Pro. The software includes all the image-editing features that you'll need. It is also able to convert files between almost every graphic format.

These pages show some of the tools available to a multimedia designer. Like any graphics software, they won't help your creative skills or turn you into an artist – but they will make it much easier to get good results.

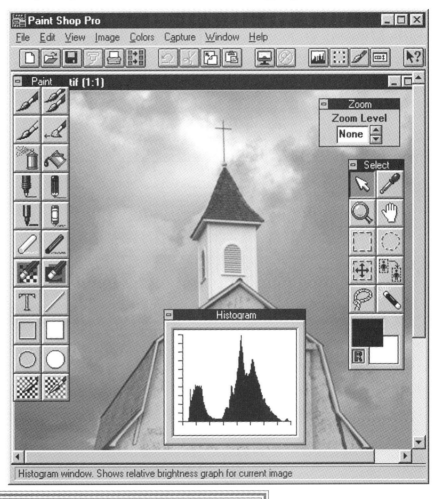

67

Photo editing software

For editing photographic-quality images, you need a more advanced program, such as Photoshop, with its powerful editing and colour-correction tools.

Advanced photo editing programs also include an 'electronic darkroom' that lets you change the contrast of parts of an image, sharpen the image or apply special filters – such as diffuser.

❑ With a powerful photo editing program you have as much control over the finished image as a photographer in a darkroom; you can darken or lighten areas, sharpen or diffuse shapes and change tones and colours.

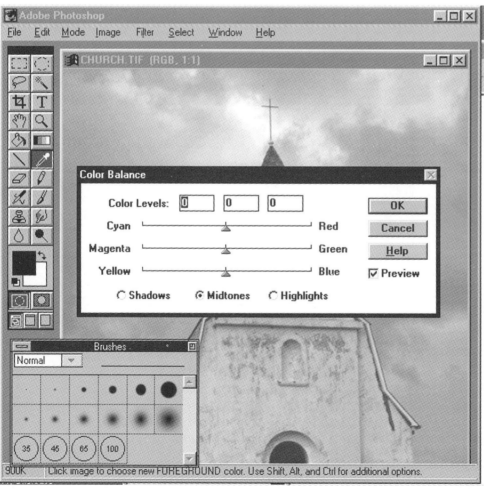

By adjusting the colour balance, you can change the mood or texture of an image

The Levels function of Photoshop displays the intensity and distribution of colours in an image.

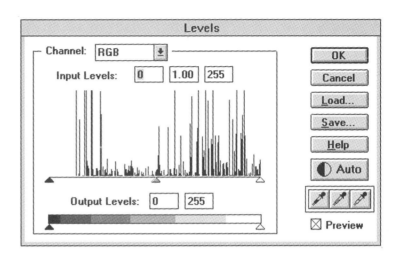

Paint Software

Paint software is now very advanced with products like Painter. This simulates different types of drawing tools – pen, brush, chalk, crayon – and also different types of paper. You can draw with a pressure sensitive tablet and the medium acts just like the real thing.

Painter's Brush Palette is illustrated here.

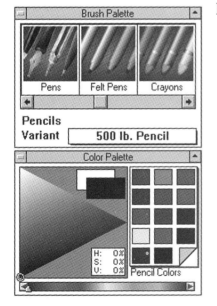

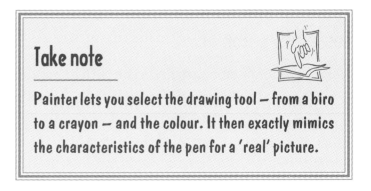

Take note

Painter lets you select the drawing tool – from a biro to a crayon – and the colour. It then exactly mimics the characteristics of the pen for a 'real' picture.

Using a scanner

A good way to convert drawings, plans or a logo into a graphics file is to use a scanner. There are many different types of scanner. The main two types are hand-held and flat-bed scanners. Hand-held scanners look rather like a fat mouse, and are dragged over the picture to capture the image (see page 19). Flat-bed scanners sit on your desk and look rather like a small photocopier.

Both types of scanner work in basically the same way: a beam of light is shone onto the image and a photo-electric detector picks up the reflection and measures its intensity. This reading represents one pixel; the beam of light passes over the entire piece of paper to convert it into a bitmap graphic file.

A flat-bed scanner is more expensive, but more accurate, as it uses a motorised beam of light rather than relying on you to drag it over the image. Both types can detect black and white, grey-scale or full colour in different resolutions.

The normal type of scanner can detect 600 dots per inch with eight-bit colour or grey-scale to give 256 different levels. It's a good idea to select a scanner that has twice the resolution of the printer you are using.

Connecting a scanner

Hand-held scanners normally come with a small interface card that fits inside your PC into an expansion slot, with a software driver, supplied on disk. A flat-bed scanner normally connects to the PC through a SCSI interface. It can simply plug into the existing controller (or the back of the CD-ROM drive) and it should work correctly.

Controlling a scanner

Many types of paint and photo-retouching software packages include support for scanners. Some DTP programs, such as Corel Ventura, also include support for a scanner. The software detects if there's a scanner installed and adds a new menu item to the menu bar.

Using scanned images

The scanner's own software lets you control the colour quality, resolution, contrast and brightness – and with a flat-bed scanner, you can also select the area to be scanned.

If the scanning software is called up from within a graphics package, the image is taken directly into the package. Once back in your graphics package, you crop the scan, resize it, rotate it, adjust its colours, or otherwise edit it to your needs. It can then be saved in the right graphic format to suit the multimedia authoring program or wordprocessor in which it will be used.

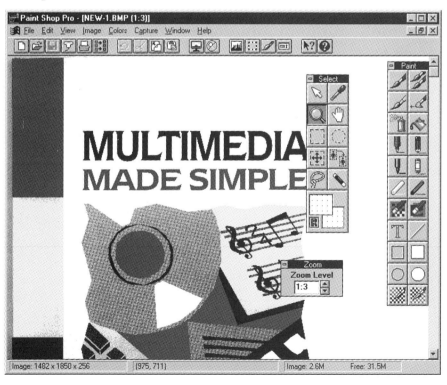

The scanner can be called up from the button in Paint Shop Pro.

Using PhotoCD

One of the most exciting new ways of capturing images to use in your multimedia programs is called Kodak PhotoCD. It's really very simple: use your normal camera to take photographs on normal film then, when you take the film to be developed, ask them to produce a PhotoCD at the same time. You'll get your prints back together with a CD-ROM at a little extra cost. The CD-ROM will contain very high-resolution, 16 million colour scans of your photographs, which you can then use in any paint program.

To read the PhotoCD you have to make sure that your CD-ROM drive is PhotoCD compatible (it should say that it is CD-XA, multisession or PhotoCD compatible).

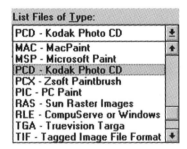

The PhotoCD includes several scans of each photograph at different resolutions and stored in various formats. This lets you test out your special effects on the smaller, low resolution images, which can be processed quickly.

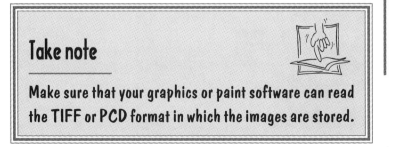

Take note

Make sure that your graphics or paint software can read the TIFF or PCD format in which the images are stored.

Basic steps

1 Take your photographs with a camera and colour film as normal.

2 Take the film to a Kodak specialist and ask for a PhotoCD as well as your prints.

3 This takes a little longer and costs more.

4 Then you get your CD-ROM, insert it into your drive.

5 Use PhotoCD access software or a graphics program to open one of the files on the disc.

❑ Once you have your photographs on PhotoCD, you can edit them or use them in a presentation.

Clip art

A good alternative if you don't have a scanner or camera is to use ready-made clip art. There are thousands of libraries of art work and photographs that you can buy or rent to use in a presentation, multimedia application or book. If you have a presentation graphics program, you'll find it has hundreds of symbols and pre-drawn artwork that you can use, modify and include in your work – from stars, flags and computers, to cars and people.

Many photographers now supply libraries of their work on disc and you can either buy the disc or buy the right to use one image for a particular project. Look in CD-ROM catalogues for clip art and photographic libraries that you can use: but make sure that you read the copyright and fee scheme first.

Different graphics software handles clip art in different ways. For example, the presentation software Harvard Graphics has a library of images that are in a special format, and can only be accessed through Harvard. You see a list of tiny representations of the images, and can paste it into your picture. Other programs supply standard clip art in TIFF, PCX or WMF (Word MetaFile) formats.

Tip

If you draw your own work, start to keep copies of the originals which you can then use at a later date and so create your own clip-art library.

Tip

If you have access to the Internet, the newsgroup alt.binaries.clip-art can be a useful source of artwork, and the comp.graphics groups have tips, discussions and images from a wide range of applications.

Summary

- You can **create your own colour images** with Paint in the Accessories group of Windows.

- **Paint** includes basic tools to edit your image, re-touch detail or change colours.

- With the Selector tools and the **Edit–Copy/Paste** commands, you can duplicate areas of your image.

- **Advanced graphics applications** turn your PC into an electronic darkroom and give you control over the contrast, colour and effects.

- To convert a picture, drawing or logo from paper to an image file use a **scanner.**

- **Hand-held scanners** are cheap, but can distort an image unless you have a steady hand.

- **Flat-bed scanners** normally connect to the same SCSI port that controls your CD-ROM, are more accurate but more expensive than a hand-held.

- If you have a camera, use the **PhotoCD** service to convert your film into colour graphic images on a CD-ROM.

- If you cannot draw, are stuck for ideas or time, use one of the **clip art** libraries and choose from the hundreds of pre-drawn symbols, maps, flags, and cartoons and other pictures.

7 Video and animation

Video

The ultimate in multimedia is to use video clips. This is more complicated than any other multimedia technology and you need a lot of expensive equipment to record video clips. The good news is that once you have recorded a video clip, anyone can play it back without needing any special equipment.

A video clip is made up of a series of separate frames, each one a single colour image and slightly different from the last. When the frames are played back fast enough, your eye sees them as continuous motion. You need to show between 15 and 25 frames every second – any less than this and the movements won't be smooth.

The frames in a video clip are colour bitmap images, so you can imagine that even a few seconds of video will take up a huge amount of disk space (ten seconds of video is equivalent to 150 frames, or 150 single image files). To cut down the space required, there are several different ways of storing the frames in a compressed format. The most popular method in Windows is called *AVI* (Audio Video Interleaved), although there is also the Apple Macintosh *QuickTime* format that runs on a Macintosh or PC.

An AVI video clip can be played by Media Player or any other video editing software. This panel shows the controls for video, sound and position in the sequence.

Any video sequence is made up of a series of separate images, each slightly different.

How it works

❏ The video card works a bit like a very high-speed sound card. When recording, it grabs each frame of video and converts this to a bitmap, then stores this on disk as one of a sequence.

❏ Once you have recorded the video signals as a series of bitmap frames, these are compressed and stored as an AVI file. AVI video files can also store sound, which is converted into a digital form in the same way that your sound card works.

❏ Video capture cards can be used either to record a video clip or to grab a single frame – this is another source of still images to use in your multimedia experiments.

Recording video

In order to record video onto your PC you will need a video capture card. This fits into an expansion slot inside your PC and connects either to a normal video camera or a VCR.

With a video card installed, you can watch the pictures it's receiving. This works through a combination of software and hardware. The software displays an empty window on the screen and colours it a special colour (called the chroma key). The video card instructs your graphics adapter to display the video images anywhere where the special colour is being displayed.

Video playback

One of the decisions you have to make when playing back a video file is the compromise between the size of the playback window and the quality of the video. Windows is not fast enough to de-compress the compressed images that make up each frame at the high resolution you need to fill the entire screen. In practice, if you want a sharp, clear image you will have to limit the area of the playback window to a few inches square.

The size of the play back window is actually determined by the speed of your PC, video card and hard disk. Windows will work this out and try and display the optimum: best picture quality at the largest window size possible.

The ultimate video system

The way to get the best quality video recording and full-screen video play back is to fit a special card. Not only will the card compress each frame in the sequence but it will work the other way around and de-compress the frames. Because there is a special processor on this card, it works much faster than Windows on your PC so you view the video in a bigger playback window and a see better quality image. The problem is the price.

The practical video system

As an alternative to using the video compression card described above, Microsoft developed Video for Windows. You still need a video capture card, but then a set of programs lets you compress a video clip and de-compress during play back through software, without requiring a special compression card. It's not quite as sophisticated as the compression card described above, and the video files take up more space on disk, but it's a lot cheaper. In fact, the software to play back video clips using Video for Windows is included free with most multimedia applications, and within the Windows 95 package is the Media Player utility which can play back AVI format files.

Video for Windows stores the video frames in the AVI file format. Once you have recorded a video clip as a standard AVI file, you can play it back within a playback window or include it in your multimedia presentation. Windows can treat a video clip like a sound file or image and embed it within another document (see page 109 for further details).

Take note

The way AVI and many other video formats store video is to only store the differences between each frame and the previous. This means that for most sequences, the size of the video file is kept smaller and the processing time is reduced.

Basic steps

Using Media Player

❏ **To play a video clip**

1 Select Start – Programs – Accessories – Multimedia – Media Player.

2 Select **File–Open** and highlight the AVI file you want to open.

The Media Player window now shows the length of the video clip and play control buttons. A new play-back window opens, with the first frame displayed.

3 Click on ▶ and the video clip will play (with sound).

The most usual way of playing a video clip is to use the Media Player utility in the Accessories–Multimedia menu. You have probably already used this flexible tool to play MIDI or sound files. It also plays back AVI-format video clips without any special hardware.

② Select an AVI file

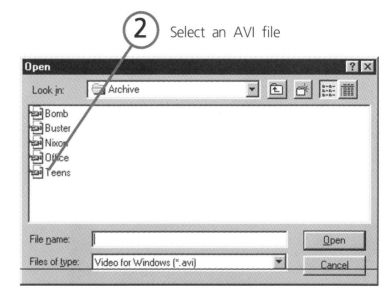

③ Click to play

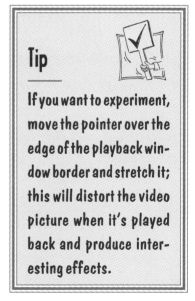

Tip

If you want to experiment, move the pointer over the edge of the playback window border and stretch it; this will distort the video picture when it's played back and produce interesting effects.

Configure playback

Media Player lets you configure some of the ways in which the video clip is displayed and played back. For example, if you are not concerned about the definition or quality of the video clip, but want a larger image, you can set Media Player to play back, filling the whole screen rather than the small default window.

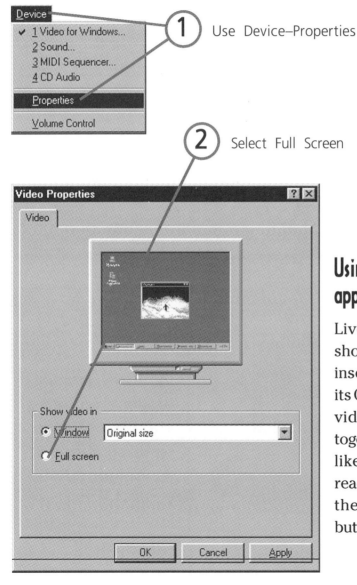

Use Device–Properties

Select Full Screen

1 Select the **Device–Properties** command.

2 In the dialog box, select the **Full Screen** option and click **OK**.

3 Press the play button. The image will be bigger, but the pixels will also be bigger.

Although called full-screen, often the video doesn't fill the entire screen, but has a black border around it – this is normal.

Using video clips in other applications

Liven up a dull report or memo with a short video clip! Windows allows you to insert an AVI file into a document using its OLE technology (see page 109). The video clip is included in your memo together with basic play controls (rather like a home video player). People reading the memo on their PCs can play the video clip by clicking on the play button.

Using a video clip

Video editing and capture software, like the Personal AVI Editor (below), allows you to manipulate an AVI video. This software lets you import images which it can convert to a video sequence – adding fade or mixing effects, or sound as required. The capture function records the signals from a video capture card (which can be connected to a camera, TV or VCR).

You need a video capture card to record video, and any accompanying sound, onto your PC's hard disk. Each frame of a sequence is only displayed for a fraction of a second before it is replaced with the next, so the capture card has to work fast. You also need a video camera or VCR with a tape of the action you want to record.

The video capture software will display whatever's 'seen' by the camera in a window on your screen. When you want to record a video clip, select the Record button. Most capture cards will also let you capture a single frame (a grab) to use as a still image.

Once you have recorded the video sequence as an AVI file, it can be played back using the Media Player or can be inserted into a presentation.

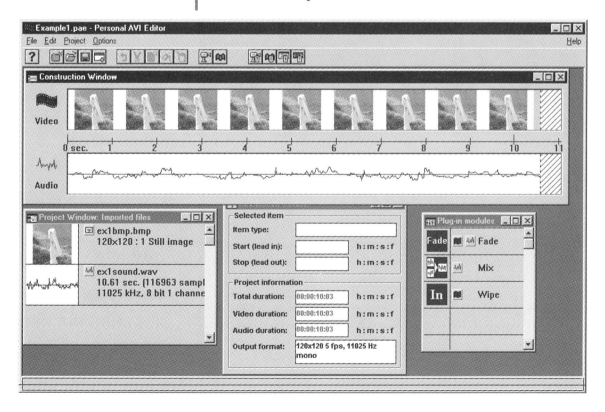

Professional video editing

With the right software, a PC can be a professional video editing suite. The editing software shown on the previous page is good for simple tasks, but for professional work, you will need to understand SMPTE which is a way of identifying each frame in a sequence. Non-professional editing software is easier to use, as each frame is numbered.

In order to cut out a frame, or create a new sequence, you enter an EDL (edit definition list). This tells the software what changes to make, for example 'delete frame 44'. The edit software will then re-build the video file looking at the EDL and making all the changes. Professional video editors work in a similar way, creating an EDL, but this is then passed to an automatic video recorder that creates a new video tape rather than a file on a PC.

Take note

If you have a video capture card, it will include editing software. Alternatively, products such as Adobe Premier provide accurate frame and sound synchronisation.

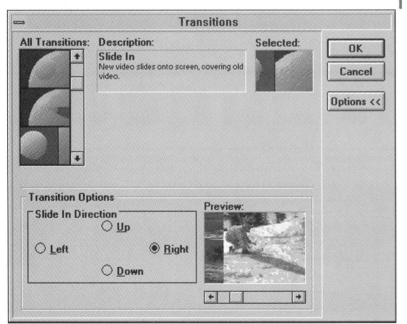

Defining a transition between two video clips, using the editor included with the Toolbook authoring software. (See Special Effects, opposite.)

Take note

To record your own video clips, you will need to buy and install a lot of extra, expensive equipment.

Video special effects

□ Video editor software also lets you create *mattes*. A matte uses two different sections of video that are blended with one video clip replacing one colour in the other clip. It's a very useful technique to create the illusion of flying or for similar effects.

To do this, you would first record a clip of someone against a plain blue background.

Next you would record a clip of a moving scene or sky. The video editor software will replace the plain blue background of the first clip with the images of the second, giving a combined effect.

The editing software normally lets you load two video clips at the same time. You can then mix these, create special effects so that one will gradually fade as the second clip appears, or cut frames from one and insert them in the other.

● A *wipe* effect is like drawing a curtain to reveal the second video under the first. It's useful for titles.

● A *dissolve* effect gradually makes the first video clip lighter while the second appears through the first.

Video editing software will also allow you to define new colours (termed the palette) for your final result and, if you need to save space, you can compress the video file.

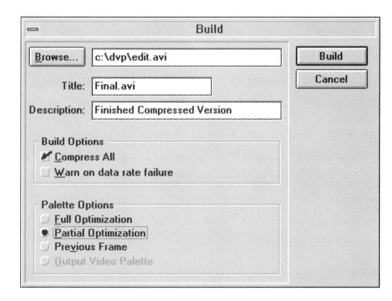

Setting the compression options before building the final version of the edited video clip.

Animation software

Video clips are not the only way to add movement and action to a multimedia presentation. A far simpler method is to use animation. It's similar to video in that a sequence of separate still images (each called a frame) is displayed rapidly in sequence and gives the impression of movement. Animation is great for moving a logo across a presentation, adding fun to an icon or to explain how something works.

A sequence of animation frames are stored in a file. There are several different file formats in which the frames can be stored. The most commonly used are the FLI, FLC and AVI formats (like the video clips described earlier).

Create an animation

For this you need special software that lets you draw an image and, over several frames, change part of it slightly so that it appears to move. For example, to make a dog run, you need to move his legs slightly in a sequence of frames and repeat the sequence over and over again.

Some animation software lets you build an animation using a cast of animated characters. Each character can move around the screen independently. Presentation software often includes a feature to move text or an image around a screen - useful if you want to gradually move a logo off the screen.

Some sophisticated animation software includes a *tweening* function. This lets you draw the starting position of an image and the end position, and the software will work out the steps and changes required to move from the first to the last, saving you a lot of time.

Tip

For smooth animation, a sequences needs to run at the same speed as a video clip: up to 25 frames per second. However, simple animation can run at 10 frames per second. As the images are often simpler, shorter and smaller than a video clip, animation files are normally much smaller.

Animation techniques

Animations are much simpler to create than you might think. And they need much less disk space and expensive equipment than video.

An animation sequence normally has a very simple or static background. This is called a *cel*. On top of the cel you place a character or actor, which can be moved according to your instructions.

The actor might have a sequence of repeated movements, perhaps to move his legs to give the impression of walking.

Setting the movement path for a unchanging object. This kind of animation is simple to do, but can be an effective way of directing people's attention towards a particular item on your multimedia page.

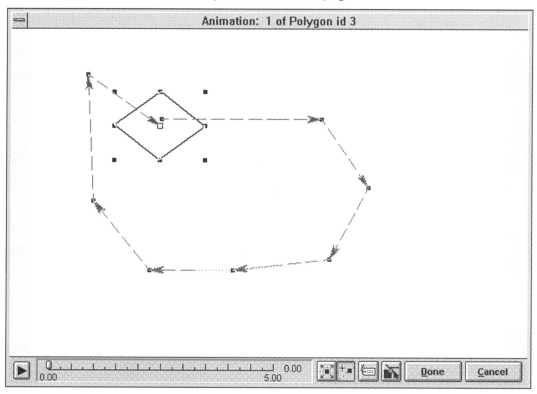

Morphing software

Morphing is a similar to the 'tweening' technique used in animation. In tweening, you define the start and end images for a character and let the software work out intermediate the stages. In morphing, the two images are normally completely different. The software then works out a sequence of steps so that the first image appears to change gradually into the second object.

It's a very effective technique if used sparingly. In the example here, a girl is transformed into a frog – and all she needs now is a prince to reverse the process.

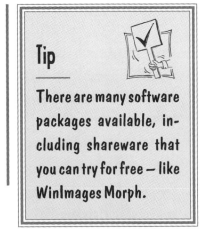

Tip

There are many software packages available, including shareware that you can try for free – like WinImages Morph.

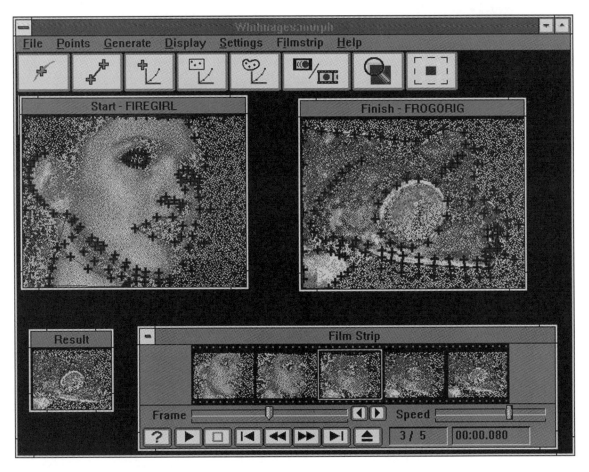

How it works

To change the girl (in the left-hand frame) into the frog (in the right-hand frame), you can specify the number of frames you want the animation sequence to span and the resolution of the final sequence.

The program works using points of reference. If you look carefully at each image, you'll see the points I have marked around the girl's and frog's heads that should be used to change the shape of the first image.

Finally, the program calculates how to change the position of the points marked and generates each frame of the finished animation.

The more frames you have, the smoother the animation.

Anti-aliasing helps to ensure a smooth colour transition

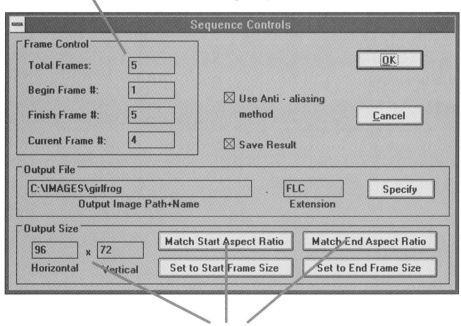

The Apect Ratio is the proportion of width to height. This may be different in the start and end frames. You can make the in-between frames to match either, or set a specific size.

Summary

❑   You can record video clips onto your hard disk by
    fitting a **video capture card** and connecting it to a
    video camera or VCR. Sound is recorded at the same
    time as movement.

❑   The video clips are made up of a **sequence of images**,
    rapidly displayed to give the impression of movement.

❑   Video clips are normally stored in the **AVI file format**.
    These can be played back on any PC and do not need
    special hardware.

❑   The **Media Player** utility in the Start – Programs –
    Accessories – Multimedia menu is used to open and
    play an AVI file.

❑   **Video editing** software normally comes with a video
    capture card or can be bought separately. It allows
    you to cut frames, change the sequence or add
    special effects.

❑   **Animation software** lets you create simple animation
    sequences that can be very effective.

❑   **Morphing** automatically animates the change of one
    image into another as a special effect.

8 Using a CD-ROM

Accessing a CD-ROM

Once you have plugged in the controller card, connected it to your CD-ROM drive and installed the software correctly (see Chapter 2), you're ready to access CD-ROMs.

The CD-ROM drive will normally appear as drive D: under DOS and Windows. If you have two hard disk drives, or are connected to a network, it might be called a different letter, but it will work in the same way.

Open the drive bay by pressing the eject button on the front of the drive. Place the CD-ROM, printed side up, onto the tray (or in the caddy) and push it back in. The drive access light will light for a few seconds, while the software checks what sort of disc you have inserted.

Once the access light has gone out, you can read data from the CD-ROM. Start Windows Explorer. On the left-hand side of the screen are listed the drives that are fitted to your PC. Click on the icon for the CD-ROM – normally drive D: and you'll see a list of files stored on the CD-ROM in the right side of the window.

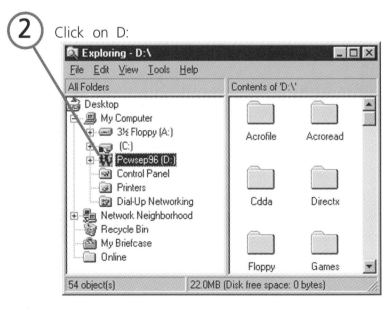

② Click on D:

❑ To copy from a CD-ROM to the hard disk

1 Load the CD-ROM, printed side up into the drive, close the tray and wait till the access light is off.

2 Run **Windows Explorer** and click on the D: icon in the drives list.

3 Explorer displays a list of the folders and files on the CD-ROM.

4 Locate the file you want to copy, click on it once and drag the file up and onto the icon for the C: drive (your hard disk).

5 Explorer will check that you want to copy the file to the C: drive. Click the **OK** button to confirm your actions.

90

Basic steps

❏ **To find a file**

1 Open the **Tools** menu and select **Find** then **Files or Folders**.

2 Enter the name of the file, or use a wildcard search pattern to find a group of related files. For example, to find all video files you would use '*.AVI'; to find all sound files you would use '*.WAV'.

3 Click **Find Now** and after a few moments, Explorer will display a list of matching files.

Searching for files on a CD-ROM

Searching for files on a CD-ROM

One of the problems with a CD-ROM is that it can store so much data – over 650Mb. If you are accessing a CD-ROM packed with clip art files, you could spend a long time searching through the folders for the one you want. Explorer includes access to the Windows Find function which is very useful when you're trying to find one file out of hundreds on a CD-ROM – or on your hard disk.

① Select Tools – Find

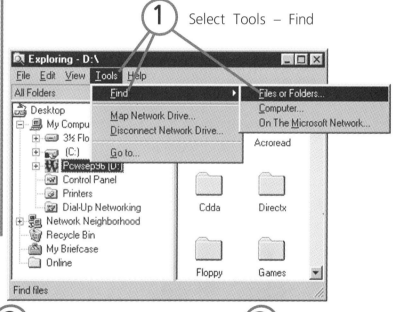

② Type in a search pattern   ③ Click Find Now

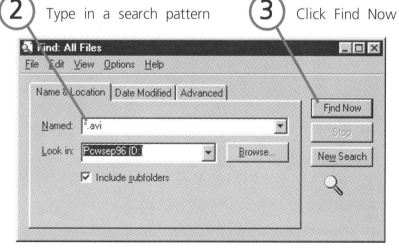

Tip

You can access the Search program from the Start button, or just press [F3] from the Desktop.

Commercial CD-ROMs

So far in this book, you've seen how multimedia works, and later you'll see how to create your own multimedia books. There are also thousands of commercial titles available that will run on your PC. When you bought your PC or CD-ROM drive (if you upgraded) you might have been given a free CD-ROM to get you started.

There is such a wide range, it's difficult to mention all of them. There are exciting games that use video, stereo sound and images to create a virtual world. Encyclopaedias are also popular, and might include text, sound, and images to bring the subject alive.

Tip

Learning becomes more interesting with multimedia. Some language courses feature video clips of the teacher, with spoken words.

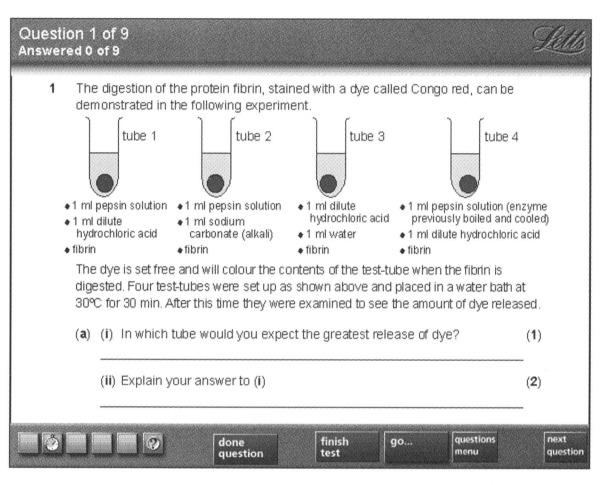

1 The digestion of the protein fibrin, stained with a dye called Congo red, can be demonstrated in the following experiment.

tube 1   tube 2   tube 3   tube 4

♦ 1 ml pepsin solution   ♦ 1 ml pepsin solution   ♦ 1 ml dilute   ♦ 1 ml pepsin solution (enzyme
♦ 1 ml dilute   ♦ 1 ml sodium   hydrochloric acid   previously boiled and cooled)
  hydrochloric acid   carbonate (alkali)   ♦ 1 ml water   ♦ 1 ml dilute hydrochloric acid
♦ fibrin   ♦ fibrin   ♦ fibrin   ♦ fibrin

The dye is set free and will colour the contents of the test-tube when the fibrin is digested. Four test-tubes were set up as shown above and placed in a water bath at 30°C for 30 min. After this time they were examined to see the amount of dye released.

(a) (i) In which tube would you expect the greatest release of dye?   (1)

_____

(ii) Explain your answer to (i)   (2)

_____

done question   finish test   go...   questions menu   next question

Multimedia titles can be very useful for training. This Letts Science revision software will simulate an exam and help with your revision.

Take note

Using multimedia is not always a passive process of reading, viewing and listening. Some titles can accept and respond to information from the user.

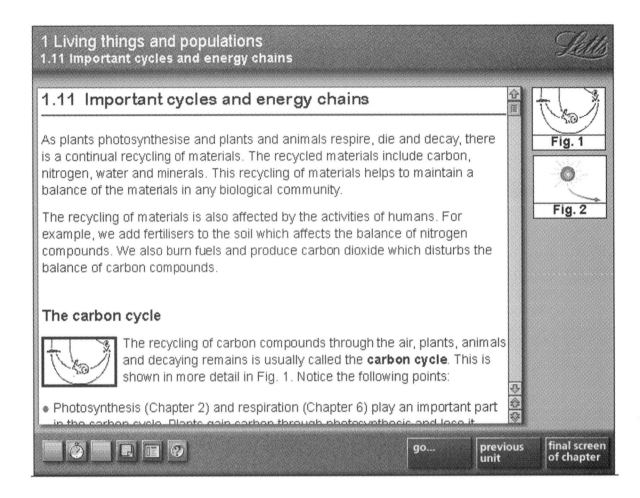

Letts

1.11 Important cycles and energy chains

As plants photosynthesise and plants and animals respire, die and decay, there is a continual recycling of materials. The recycled materials include carbon, nitrogen, water and minerals. This recycling of materials helps to maintain a balance of the materials in any biological community.

The recycling of materials is also affected by the activities of humans. For example, we add fertilisers to the soil which affects the balance of nitrogen compounds. We also burn fuels and produce carbon dioxide which disturbs the balance of carbon compounds.

The carbon cycle

The recycling of carbon compounds through the air, plants, animals and decaying remains is usually called the **carbon cycle**. This is shown in more detail in Fig. 1. Notice the following points:

● Photosynthesis (Chapter 2) and respiration (Chapter 6) play an important part

Fig. 1

Fig. 2

go...   previous unit   final screen of chapter

In the Letts revision titles, you first find your weak areas with the exam simulator, then use its encyclopedia to find the information you need to be able to answer the questions.

Place bookmarks to return
quickly to selected items

The Zoom control lets you set the balance
of print size and amount displayed

Type in a word...   ... or scroll through
the list

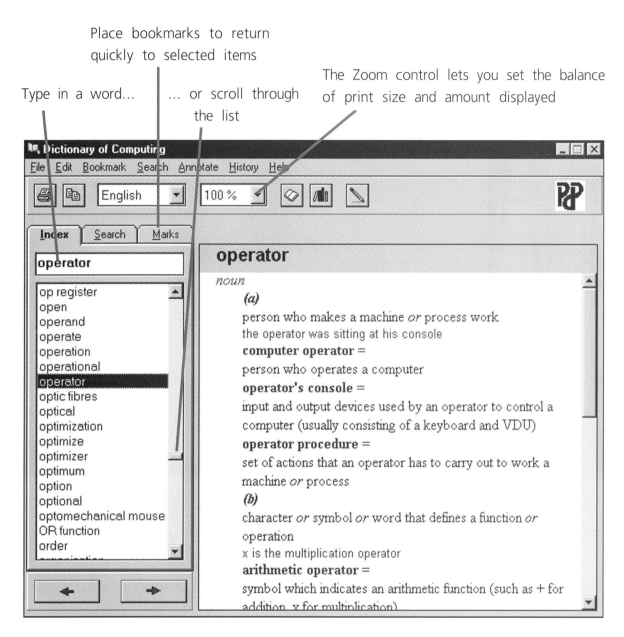

Titles such as this computer dictionary from PCP squeeze the entire
text of a large book into a CD-ROM and include links between
words, as well as having search functions.

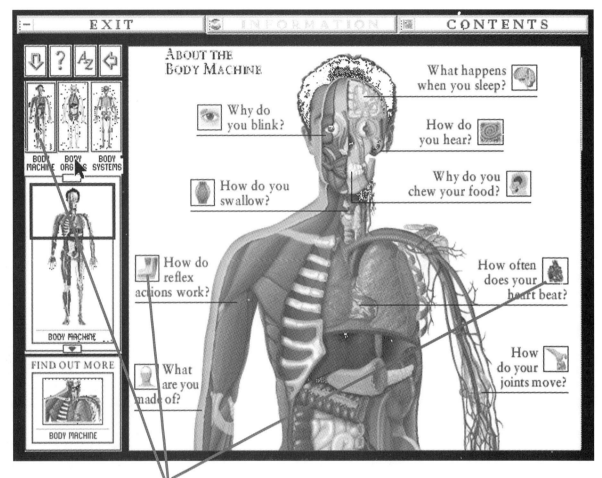

Clicking on the pictures take you to the related pages

Dorling Kindersley's 'How the Human Body Works' uses hotspots (see page 103) to link graphics and text to great effect.

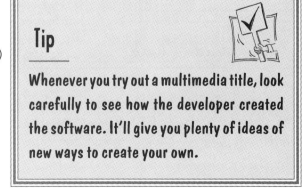

Tip

Whenever you try out a multimedia title, look carefully to see how the developer created the software. It'll give you plenty of ideas of new ways to create your own.

Anglia's Seashore Life works in a very different way from the Lett's Science (pages 93-94). Instead of asking questions and processing answers, it lets the user explore by clicking on objects on the page to find out more.

Starfish

You can see starfish in rock pools. They like to feed on mussels which also live there. The starfish pulls apart the mussel shell with its tube feet.

HELP

Programs from CD-ROMs

When you buy an application program on a CD-ROM, you must install it before it can be used. With Windows 95 software there is usually a Setup program on the CD-ROM. This copies configuration files onto your hard disk and creates a new program group and icon.

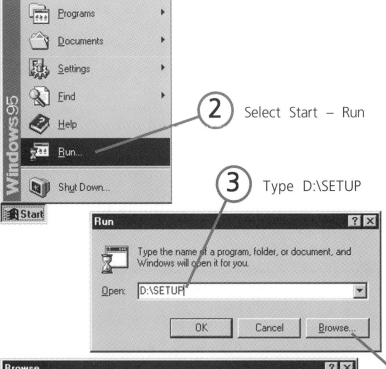

Select Start – Run

Type D:\SETUP

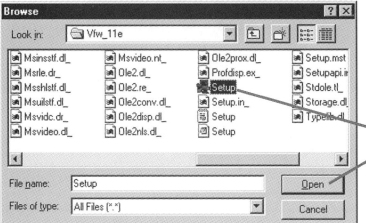

Click Browse

Open the program

1 Ensure the CD-ROM is in the drive and the access light is off.

2 Select the **Run** option from the **Start** menu.

3 Type in 'D:\SETUP' – change the drive letter to suit your PC – and click **OK**.

4 The program should install the software onto your hard disk.

5 If it doesn't work, type in the CD-ROM drive letter and click **Browse**.

6 Find a file called 'INSTALL', 'SETUP' or something similar and click **Open**.

Limited installations

Some multimedia programs give you a choice: either copy the files onto your hard disk, which takes up a lot of disk space, or keep them mostly on the CD-ROM disc, which means that access to the files is slower.

Many of the multimedia encyclopedias will only copy a small program file onto the hard disk, keeping the hundreds of Megabytes of data on the CD-ROM.

Smaller applications, such as authoring tools, dictionaries and music packages, will give you the option to copy the larger data files onto the hard disk.

● If you don't use the software very often, choose the second option or you'll use up all your free disk space.

● If the software runs very slowly, try re-installing it onto your hard disk which will be much faster.

Take note

AutoPlay is one Windows 95's great features. It can detect when you have inserted a CD-ROM into the drive. If the CD-ROM's setup software has been written to use AutoPlay, Windows will automatically install and start the software.

When installing new software, you might want to set your own Destination DIrectory – perhaps to store the software on a second hard drive, or so that you do not overwrite an earlier version of the same program.

99

Installing application software

When you install application software that helps you develop multimedia titles, edit music or create graphics, there are often choices that define the parts of the application to install.

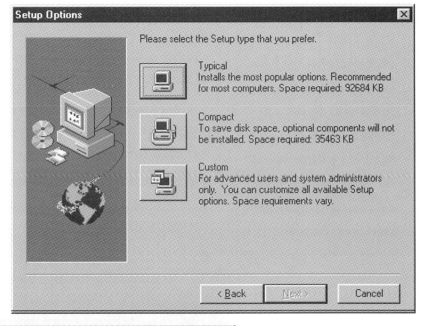

This graphics designer package gives you the option to install the parts of the software that you need.

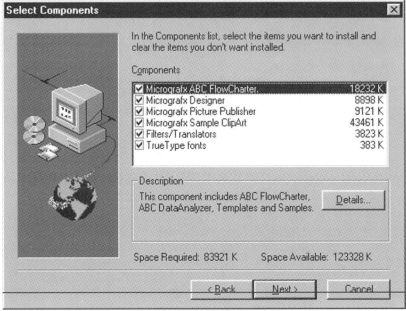

With the Micrografx package, you can save over 40Mb of disk space by not installing the ClipArt – will you really use it?

You can always reinstall software, to add more components, if you find you need them at a later date.

Basic steps

1 Open the **Control Panel** with **Start – Settings**.

2 Double-click the **Add/ Remove** icon.

3 Highlight the program entry from the list.

4 Click the **Add/Remove** button to remove the software.

Tip

Windows 95 software is normally supplied with an UNINSTALL utility to remove the application when it is no longer wanted.

Removing software

If you want to remove a multimedia title or application from your hard disk, you can use the uninstall feature which is part of any Windows 95 compatible software.

● Some software will add an icon to the program group – often labelled Uninstall or Remove.

● If there is no icon, you can use the feature built-in to the Control Panel.

③ Highlight the program

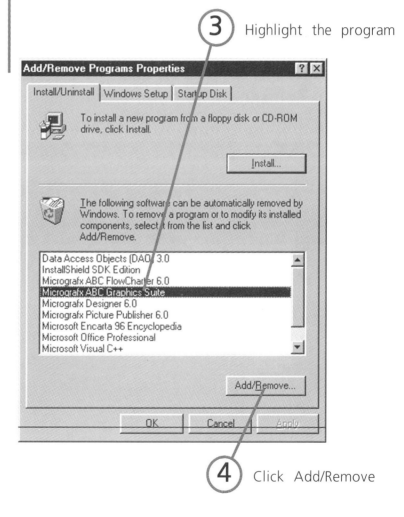

④ Click Add/Remove

Hypertext

Trying to use a new multimedia title for the first time is not as difficult as it might seem. All titles have similar functions and follow similar conventions for the user-interface.

The design of a screen might be very complex, fancy or very stark, but the way in which you interact with the software is unlikely to vary.

If there is any text on screen, you might see certain words displayed in a different colour or underlined. These are *hot-words*, and they have *hypertext* links to other information. This could be as simple as a little box that pops up to explain a complex term, or it could take you to a different page in the title.

Basic steps

1 Look for hot-words – these are underlined or displayed in a different colour.

2 Move the pointer over the word – it should change shape to look like a hand.

3 With the hand pointer over the hot-word, click once on the left button and see what is linked to the word.

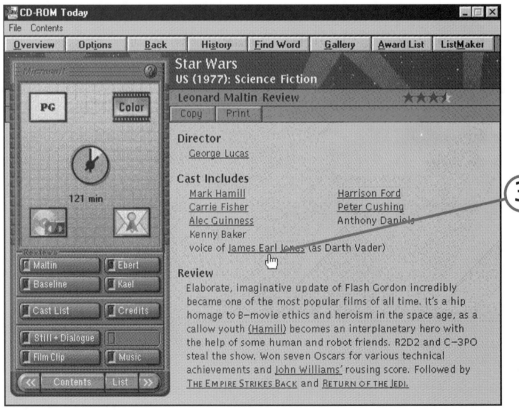

Basic steps

1 Move your pointer over a picture and see if the pointer changes shape.

2 If it changes to a hand, you are over a hotspot. This could be part of a picture or an entire picture.

3 When you are over a hotspot, click once with the left button to start the action.

Hotspots

A *hotspot* is very similar to a hot-word, but is an area of a picture. For example, if you have a multimedia title describing a violin, the image of the violin might be a hotspot. When you click on the violin, it carries out some action: maybe playing a violin sound, or displaying more detailed information.

Take note

Hotspots are not necessarily easy to see. Watch for the hand pointer.

② In this title each window is a hot spot

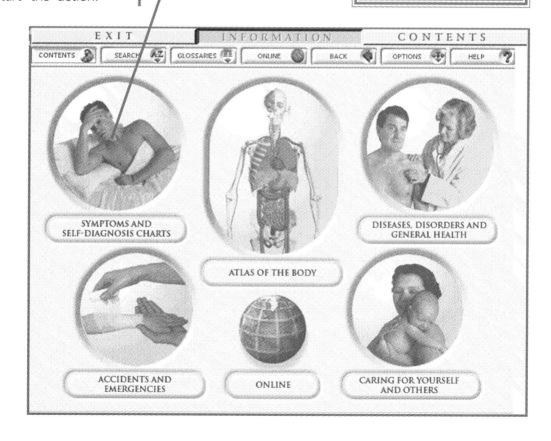

Buttons

Buttons are an obvious way of interacting with a multi-media application. You might be used to normal, grey square buttons in Windows, but a button in a multimedia application can be any shape or colour.

They is normally a caption telling you what the button will do, though if the multimedia application has a very modern design, the buttons might just have symbols and no caption text. Some symbols are easy to recognise from other Windows applications:

 open a file

 search

other symbols are not so common, for example:

 to exit the software

 move to the next page in the multimedia book

❏ **To select a button**

1 Look for a 3-D effect shape with caption text or a symbol.

2 Move the pointer over the caption or symbol – it might change shape to look like a hand.

3 With the hand pointer over the button, click once on the left mouse button and you will start the action.

Tip

If you're not sure what a button does, move the pointer over the button and wait a couple of seconds. Most Windows 95 programs will display a tiny caption for the button. Other programs will display a description in a status bar.

Searching

If the multimedia software contains information, rather than being just a game, you will almost certainly be able to search the file for key words. There are different ways of starting the search function: some programs will use a button, others a menu option.

Once you have opened the search window, you can either type in a word you want to find, or a more complex search sentence. For a simple search, just enter the word and click on OK. For more complex searches, you can use special words called logical operators. These are: AND, OR, NOT and are used between words.

For example, if you want to search for any page that has the words 'mouse' and 'cheese' you would type in:

'mouse AND cheese'.

If you want to make the search more specific, perhaps to exclude any pages that also have the word 'cat', then you would type in

'mouse AND cheese NOT cat'.

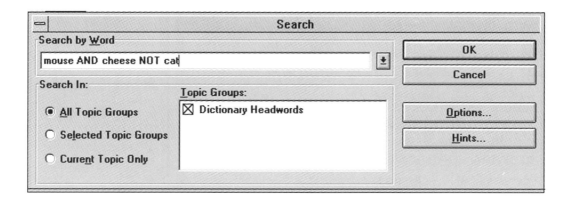

Summary

❑ Your CD-ROM drive will normally appear as drive D: under **Explorer**.

❑ Use the **Tools – Find** menu option of Explorer to find files on a CD-ROM.

❑ There are thousands of **commercial titles** available from games to clip art, teaching, encylopaedias and dictionaries. Look at how they were designed to get ideas for your own production.

❑ When you **install the software**, some files are copied to your hard disk (for speed), but the bulk remain on the CD-ROM.

❑ Many new programs will automatically install and run the program when you insert the CD-ROM.

❑ When you **run the software**, you normally have to keep the CD-ROM in the drive.

❑ **Hot-words** are used to link to another page or display extra information. They are displayed in a different colour. The pointer changes to a hand when over a hot-word.

❑ **Hotspots** are similar to hot-words, but are parts of an image.

❑ **Buttons** might look like normal Windows buttons or could be any shape with text or a symbol.

❑ To narrow down a **search**, use the special logical operators AND, OR, NOT.

9 Creating multimedia

Multimedia data

Now that you have explored how multimedia works, you can start using it to make your everyday documents, memos and messages more interesting. This chapter shows you how to use the tools provided with Windows to add sound to a memo and a video clip to a catalogue.

These are simple but very effective uses of multimedia. If you plan to carry out a lot of presentations, you should consider buying special presentation software, as described on page 119.

Creating a multimedia catalogue in WordPad (see page 113)

Take note

To create multimedia applications, you need an authoring package, that lets you create hotspots, hot-words and links to other pages.

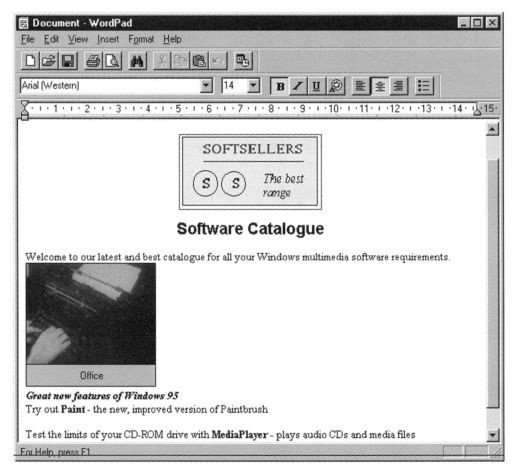

Basic steps

❏ **to add a sound**

1 Run **WordPad** and start typing your memo.

2 Place the cursor at the point where you want to add a sound.

3 Select **Insert – Object.**

4 From the list of objects, select **Wave sound**.

5 Check **Create New.**

Cont...

Multimedia objects

Windows includes a very powerful feature called OLE (object linking and embedding). This allows any Windows application to use data from almost any other Windows application. For example, if you are typing a memo in WordPad, you can insert an object created with the Sound Recorder.

It's a great way of livening up a memo or of adding personal spoken notes to explain a spreadsheet or meeting. Of course, you cannot print a sound! So this method works best if you have a network to distribute your files or can send a memo via electronic mail.

Start WordPad

Leave the cursor where the sound will go

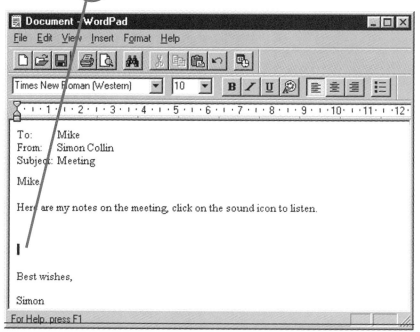

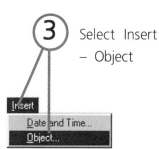
Select Insert – Object

..cont

6 Sound Recorder starts – record your message.

7 Select Exit & Return to save your sound.

8 A speaker icon will appear in your WordPad document.

❑ To play the sound file, double-click on the speaker icon.

(5) Create New   (4) Select Wave Sound

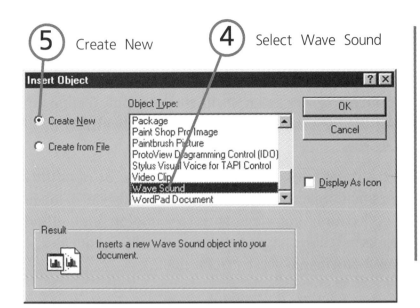

(7) Exit from Recorder

(8) Look for the speaker

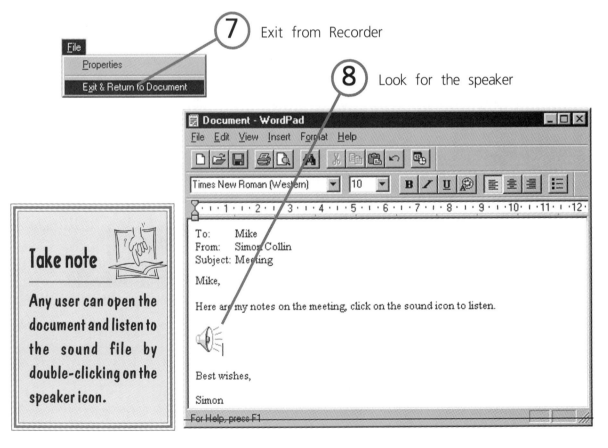

Take note

Any user can open the document and listen to the sound file by double-clicking on the speaker icon.

110

Basic steps

1 In your WordPad document, position the cursor where the picture is to go.

2 Select the **Insert – Object** menu option.

3 Scroll through the list of OLE objects and select **Paintbrush picture**.

4 Click **OK**. Windows will automatically start Paint – within WordPad.

Cont...

You've seen how to insert a sound into a memo. Using this technique, you can add a picture to a letter. It might be a company logo at the top, or your signature at the bottom of a form letter used for a mail-shot.

To show how to add a picture we will embed the signature within the letter

Painting your signature is easy with the Paint program, (see page 55 for more on Paint).

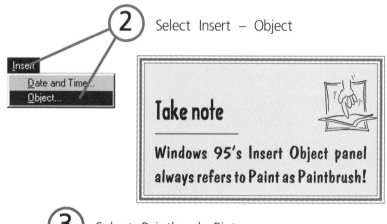

② Select Insert – Object

Take note

Windows 95's Insert Object panel always refers to Paint as Paintbrush!

Tip

If you don't fancy trying to write your signature with the mouse, scan it on from paper and save it as a bitmap. You can then insert it using the Create from File option.

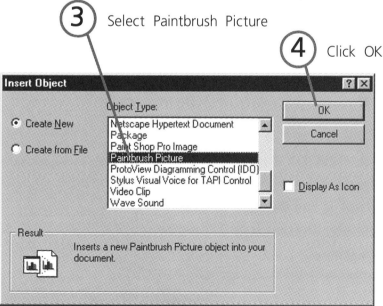

③ Select Paintbrush Picture

④ Click OK

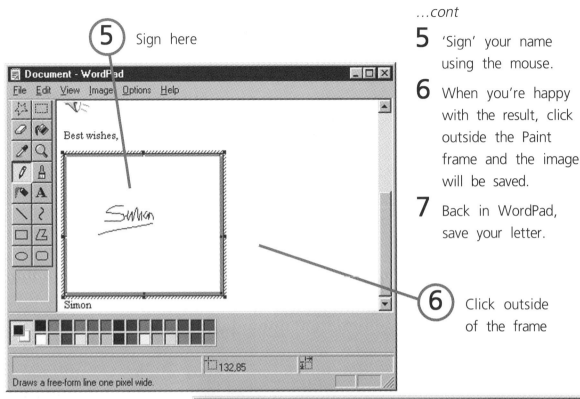

(5) Sign here

...cont

5 'Sign' your name using the mouse.

6 When you're happy with the result, click outside the Paint frame and the image will be saved.

7 Back in WordPad, save your letter.

(6) Click outside of the frame

(6) Save your file

Tip

If you ever want to edit the signature image, double-click on it within WordPad and Windows will start Paint and load the picture.

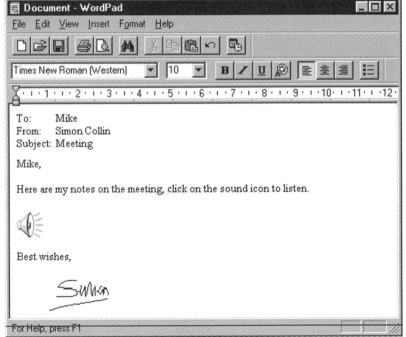

112

Basic steps

1 Start WordPad – this will be the foundation for the multimedia catalogue.

2 Type in the basic text for the catalogue and format the heading.

3 Position the cursor at the top of the page, where you will add your company logo.

4 Select **Insert – Object** and scroll through the list till you reach Paint, then click **OK**.

If you put together all the elements you've learnt so far in this chapter you can make an eye-catching catalogue that combines video, sound and pictures. All this through the simple WordPad program, which means you can experiment with multimedia without having to spend any more money on expensive development software.

To create the catalogue, we will use the OLE functions described in the last few pages. When you added your signature to the letter you will have seen the list of multimedia objects that you can embed within WordPad – and this is exactly how we'll add the video clips.

Take note

When you are creating text with WordPad, you can use any font from the Format–Font menu option.

3 Position the cursor

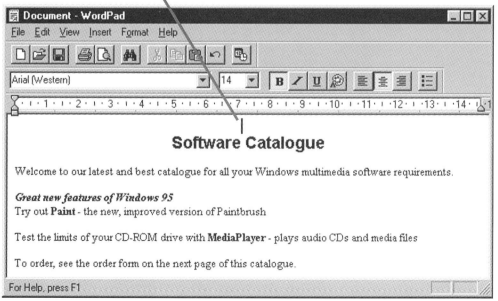

Software Catalogue

Welcome to our latest and best catalogue for all your Windows multimedia software requirements.

Great new features of Windows 95
Try out **Paint** - the new, improved version of Paintbrush

Test the limits of your CD-ROM drive with **MediaPlayer** - plays audio CDs and media files

To order, see the order form on the next page of this catalogue.

⑤ Draw your logo

⑥ Embed it

...cont

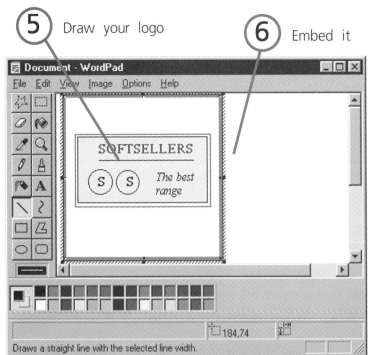

5 In Paint, draw your company logo.

6 Click out of the frame to embed the image into your document.

7 Now to add a video clip. Place the cursor where it is to go.

8 Select **Insert – Object**, then **Media Clip** and click **OK**.

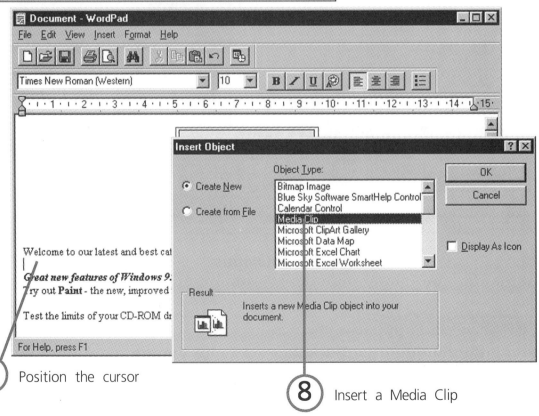

⑦ Position the cursor

⑧ Insert a Media Clip

114

9 In Media Player, select **Insert Clip – Video** and load the video clip file.

10 Click outside the frame to embed the video.

9 Open the clip file

10 Embed it

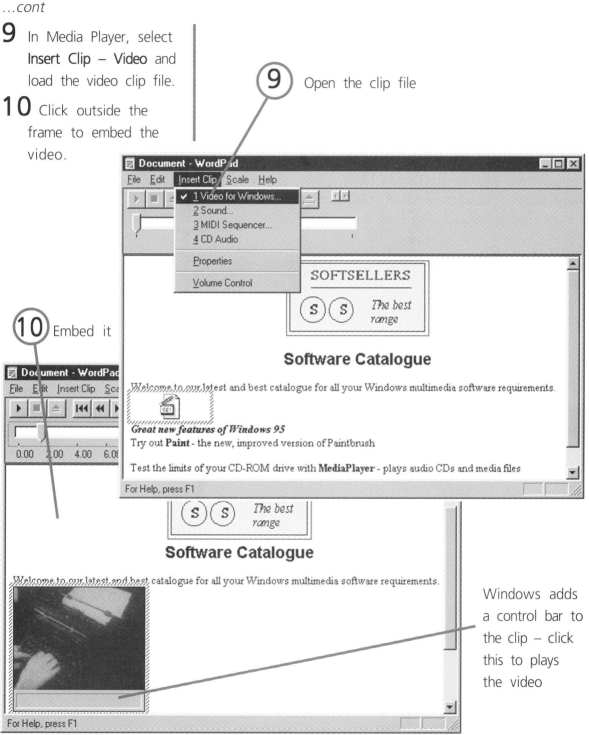

Windows adds a control bar to the clip – click this to plays the video

115

Advanced applications

More sophisticated programs, such as Microsoft Word, include a macro language. This lets you program functions into the software. You could create a special order form in Word or a fax cover sheet – you can even create complex multimedia applications.

Most macro languages let you add buttons to a document and also move between pages. If you link these two features, you can mimic the functions of a multimedia authoring tool and let your users move through pages by clicking on a button. Each page could have a picture of a different product or a video or sound clip.

Take note

WordPad doesn't have a macro language, so you can't do anything too clever with it!

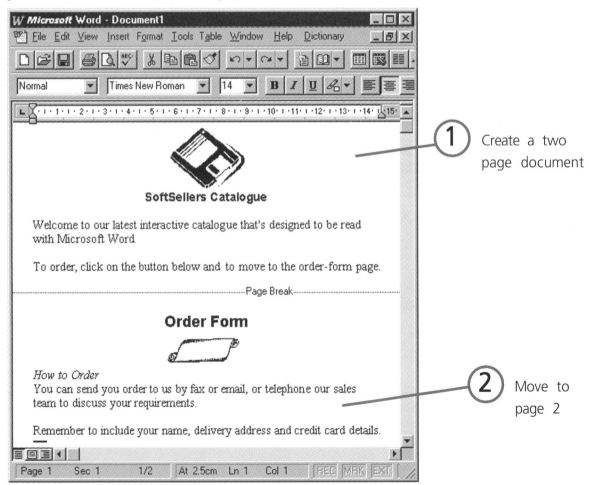

① Create a two page document

② Move to page 2

116

Basic steps

❏ Authoring in Word

1 Create two pages of text, add graphic images or embed video clips.

2 Move to the second page.

3 Select the **Edit— Bookmark** function.

4 Type in 'page2' as the bookmark name and click **Add**.

Cont...

Take note

This example will work with Microsoft Word for Windows. If you use a different Windows word-processor, check which commands it uses to add a bookmark and move between pages.

Using MS-Word

The pages are each given a unique *bookmark*–a named place on a page within the Word document.

Word's macro language includes the '*gotobutton*' command. This will create a hot-word that, when selected, will move the user to the named bookmark.

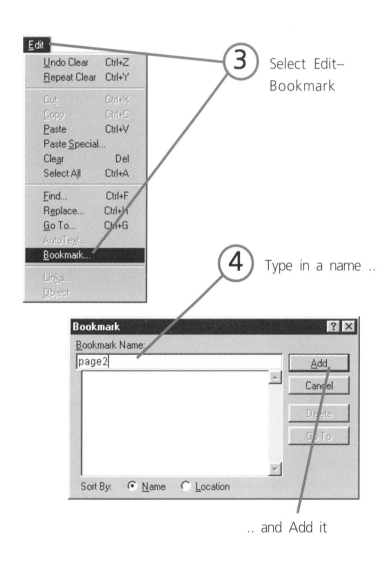

3 Select Edit– Bookmark

4 Type in a name ..

.. and Add it

... cont

6 Choose GoToButton

9 Click OK

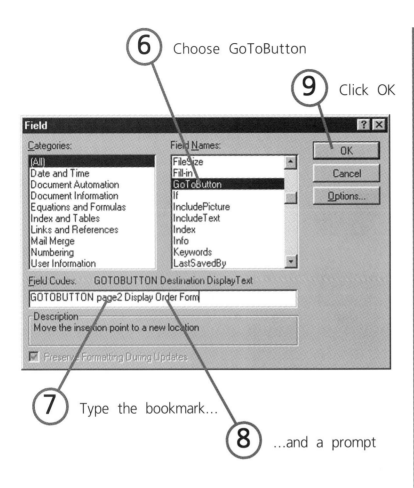

7 Type the bookmark...

8 ...and a prompt

5 Move to the first page, position the cursor where you want the button and select the **Insert–Field** menu option.

6 Scroll down through the **Field Names** list on the right and choose **GoToButton**.

7 In the **Field Codes:** slot, enter 'page2' after the GOTOBUTTON key word.

8 Now type a prompt to appear in the document.

9 Click **OK**.

❏ The prompt will be displayed on page 1 of your document. When a user double-clicks on its text, the macro will be move the current position to the bookmark 'page2' that is on the second page – in effect, turning over a page.

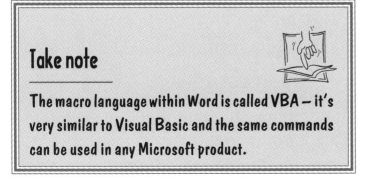

Take note

The macro language within Word is called **VBA** – it's very similar to **Visual Basic** and the same commands can be used in any **Microsoft** product.

118

General rules

Creating a presentation

❑ When designing a presentation follow these simple rules to make it as clear and effective as possible.

1 Try and **use a uniform background** to all your slides. Add your logo to reinforce the company image.

2 Don't use **too many typefaces**, no more than two per slide.

3 Don't have **more than five lines of text** on points for any slide, or your audience will get bored.

4 Make **graphs simple and clear**, two simple graphs are better than one complex one.

5 Don't use **too many colours or special effects** and try and maintain consistent look to each slide.

6 **Print handout**, based on the slides, to give to your audience.

There are dozens of special software packages that will simplify the task of creating business presentations to use when pitching for a new account, displaying sales figures or company results.

A presentation is made up of separate *slides*, and each slide can include text, graphics or graphs. Typically, it would start with a title slide, then move to one displaying with the contents, and then show slides of figures, graphs or important points.

Presentation software is now very advanced and lets you create a master slide for the entire show (see page 120). This might have your company logo in one corner and perhaps a uniform background picture or colour. Each separate slide is then created from your existing database. To help your audience, you can print out the slides so that they can make notes and keep a record of your talk.

This slide uses bullet points and a clip art image to get its message across.

Using presentation software

Presentation software provides all the functions you need to prepare professional-looking slides. The software should combine a paint-package with simple multimedia functions. To start your presentation, define the 'master' slide. This is the background that will be used for all the slides throughout your presentation. You could draw your company's logo using the Paint software, or scan in existing artwork.

Once you have the master slide, type in the text for your presentation. If you need to use data from a spreadsheet (to show company results), the presentation software will let you import the data and create a graph.

The finished sequence can be viewed as a slide show. You can set the presentation software to either display each slide for a fixed time before moving onto the next slide, or you can move on one slide by clicking the mouse button.

Tip

Remember to use the spell-check feature of your presentation software – there's nothing worse that mistakes in your presentation!

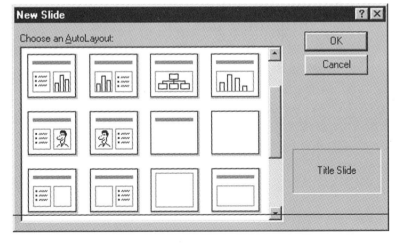

Presentation software normally includes a wide range of time-saving templates – both for single slide layouts (see left) and for whole presentations.

Basic steps

PowerPoint

1 Start PowerPoint. Select the option to use a wizard to setup a new presentation.

2 The wizard will ask about the type of presentation you want to create.

3 Enter the name of the speaker and the subject he will be discussing.

Microsoft PowerPoint provides all the features that you are likely to need for a presentation. It is supplied with Microsoft Office, so you might already have it installed on your computer!

Creating a new presentation

PowerPoint includes a wizard that helps you create presentations quickly and easily. The wizard does all the hard work of selecting background images, formatting text and placing images, leaving you to think about the information in the presentation.

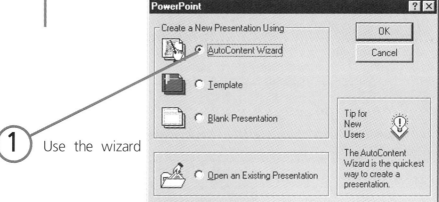

① Use the wizard

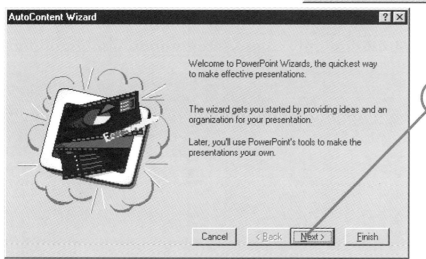

② Respond to the prompts and click Next after each stage

121

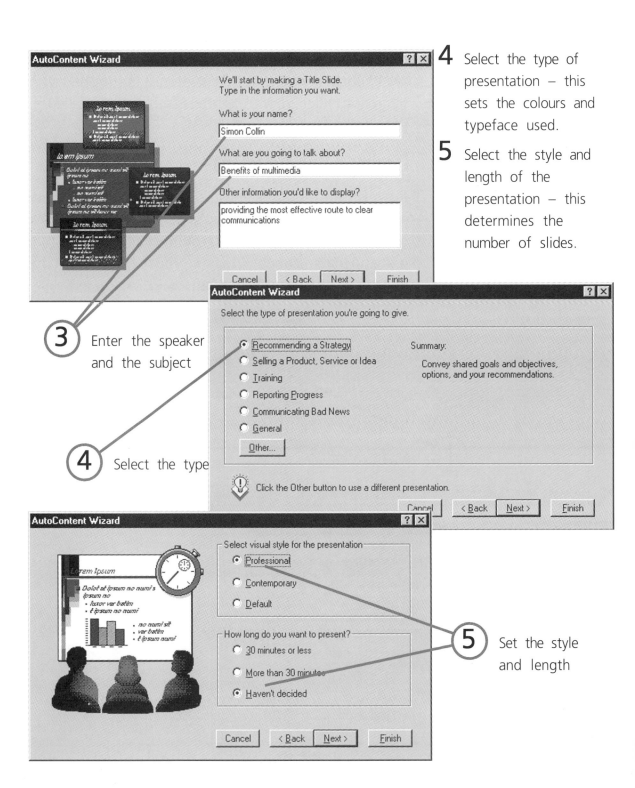

4 Select the type of presentation – this sets the colours and typeface used.

5 Select the style and length of the presentation – this determines the number of slides.

③ Enter the speaker and the subject

④ Select the type

⑤ Set the style and length

6 Select how the slides will be used.

❑ The wizard will now create the set of formatted slides

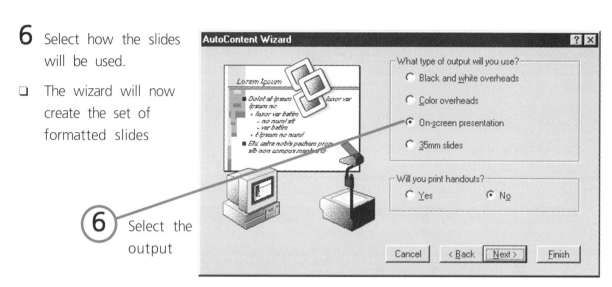

6 Select the output

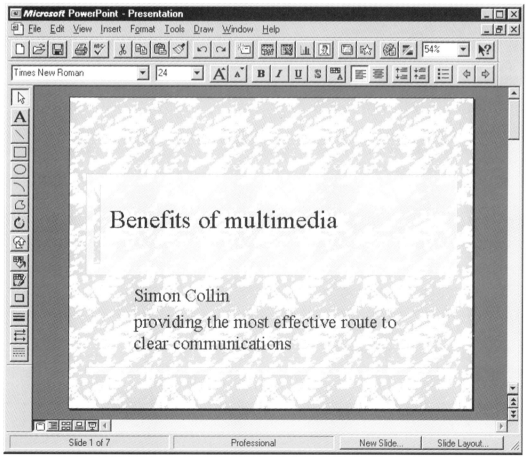

8 Select the **View – Outline** command to see the headings of each slide and to edit the dummy text that the wizard has included.

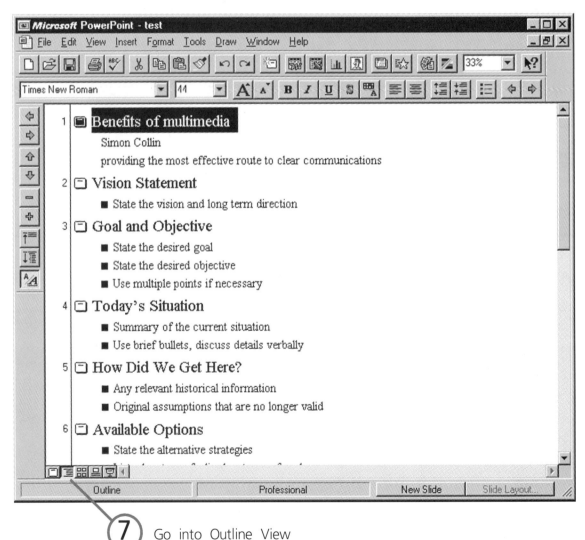

1 **Benefits of multimedia**
   Simon Collin
   providing the most effective route to clear communications

2 **Vision Statement**
   ■ State the vision and long term direction

3 **Goal and Objective**
   ■ State the desired goal
   ■ State the desired objective
   ■ Use multiple points if necessary

4 **Today's Situation**
   ■ Summary of the current situation
   ■ Use brief bullets, discuss details verbally

5 **How Did We Get Here?**
   ■ Any relevant historical information
   ■ Original assumptions that are no longer valid

6 **Available Options**
   ■ State the alternative strategies

⑦ Go into Outline View

124

Authoring software

The greatest challenge, and the best way of displaying your creative talents, is to develop your own multimedia title. This is not as difficult as you might think and with a little effort and a good idea, you can rival many commercial CD-ROMs.

Take note

If you want to distribute or sell your new multimedia title to other users, some authoring packages charge a fee, others let you do this for free.

We seen that it is possible to create a simple multimedia catalogue, just using the tools supplied with Windows. However, WordPad is not flexible nor powerful enough to manage more complex titles, of the sort that combine dozens of different pages, images, text, audio and perhaps video clips. Just like a commercial application, you will have to program hotspots, hot-words and buttons that a user can use to move between pages and get the most from your title.

There are many different types of authoring packages available, varying in price and in how difficult they are to learn. Surprisingly, some of the cheapest are also the simplest to use – mainly because they don't have hundreds of complex features that only a programmer could use.

Types of packages

There are three main types of authoring package.

One uses a *script language* in which the developer (you) writes out instructions to place images and video clips on a page and define how they react to a user. These types of package are powerful because it is possible to do just about anything with them – but they take time to learn. If you want your title to be able to react to information typed in by the user, you really need to look at a script-based authoring package.

Icon-based packages can be as powerful as script-based packages, but are much simpler for non-programmers to use. Actions are represented by icons. You first create pages by placing your images and text, then you define how they react to a user with the action icons.

The third type is stage-based. Macromedia Director, see opposite, is a good example of this type

Designing a title

To create your own multimedia title using an icon-based authoring package is easy – but you have to plan ahead carefully to avoid problems.

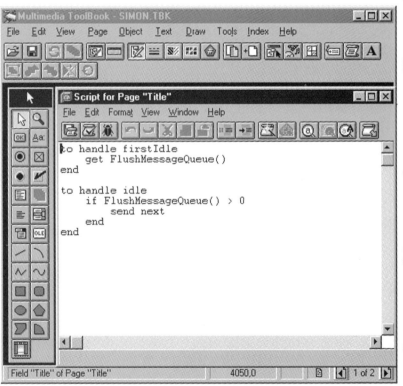

You create titles in Multimedia Toolbook by writing scripts

1 Sketch the layout of each page in the book.

2 Compile a list of all the resources you need: the text, images, sounds, icons, and video clips.

3 Record all the sounds, edit them and add any special effects.

4 Create the graphics.

5 Type in the text and note where you want to include hot-words.

6 Use the authoring software to design the pages, include the buttons to move between the pages.

7 Import and place the sounds, images and text you've prepared.

8 Use the authoring functions to define how the title reacts to the user's actions.

9 Sit back and play your finished title.

Macromedia Director

The Director window is full of tools – with a paint package on the right, list of cast members in the middle, overall control at the bottom left and the script at the top of the window.

Macromedia Director is one of the most popular tools available. This time, Director treats the title as if it were a film. Each page is a different set and there is a cast of buttons, text, images and sound. You combine all these together using the script that tells Director when to display various objects – for example, display an image on the first page and again on the fourth.

Director is an excellent design tool for anyone who wants to create interactive titles, but it is not quite as flexible as a script-based package when it comes to processing information that a user has typed in.

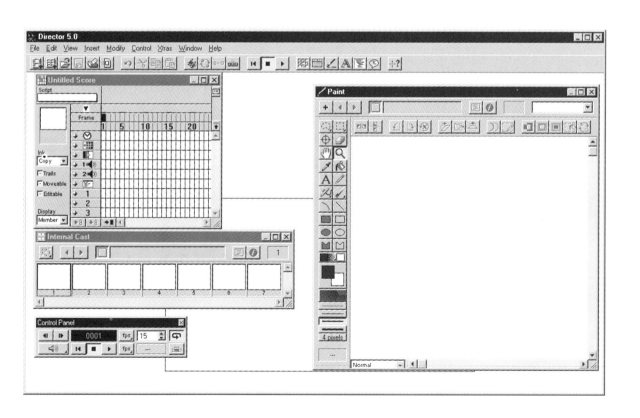

Creating an interactive title

It is easy to create a multimedia title that displays page after page of images and text, but this would be more like a presentation than a multimedia title.

To make a title interesting, it must be interactive and allow the user enter information, get feedback and control what happens and the pages he visits. Many commercial titles use hot spots within the pages that play a sound, display explanatory text or show an animation. The user can then explore the title and move through it the way he wants to.

Here we'll create a complete, but very simple, interactive multimedia title. It will only have one page, but it shows the different elements that are used in almost all titles. The project is to create a title that helps teach children the time. If the child clicks on the correct time, they'll hear applause. To create this, I have used Asymetrix Toolbook.

1 Find a suitable clock image, or scan one in and edit it in **Paint Shop Pro** or other graphics package.

2 Start the **Toolbook** authoring program.

3 Select the **File – Import Graphic** menu option.

4 The image of the clock is displayed – move and size the image by dragging the re-size handles at its corners to place it in the centre of the screen.

5 Select the text tool and drag to create an area. Double-click on this and type in the text 'What time is it?'.

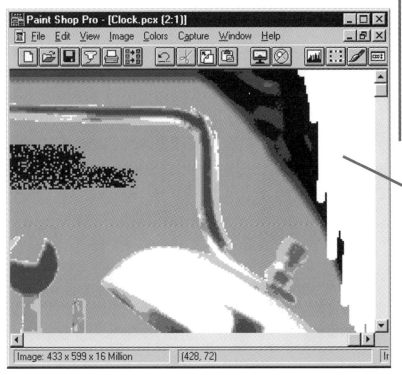

① Editing the image in Paint Shop Pro

6 Now to add a hot spot to the clock. The easiest way is to use a drawing tool.

7 Draw a square over the correct hour on the clock (10 in this case).

5 Use the text tool to add a question

6 Select a drawing tool

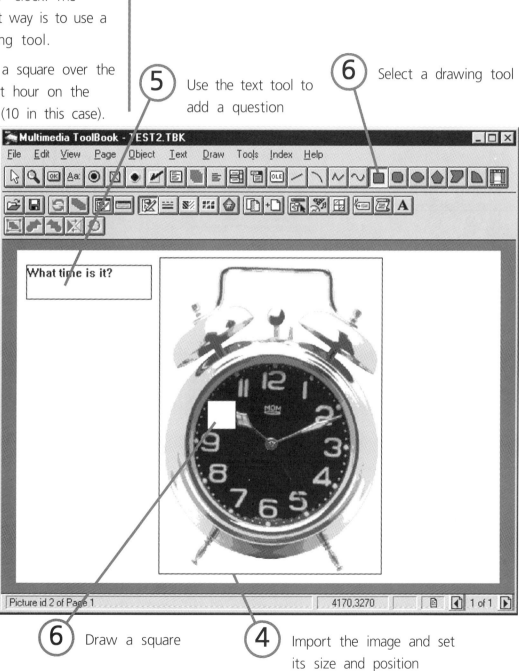

6 Draw a square

4 Import the image and set its size and position

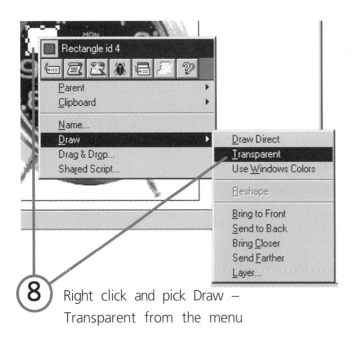

Right click and pick Draw –
Transparent from the menu

8 Right click on the
square and choose
Draw – Transparent to
hide the square and
show the clock.

9 Double-click on the
transparent square and
select the script editor
icon button.

10 Select the **Edit – Insert
Auto Script** option and
choose the **Play a Wave
File** script command.
Enter the name of the
WAV sound file you
want to play.

11 Click **OK** to paste this
command into the
square.

9 Open the script editor

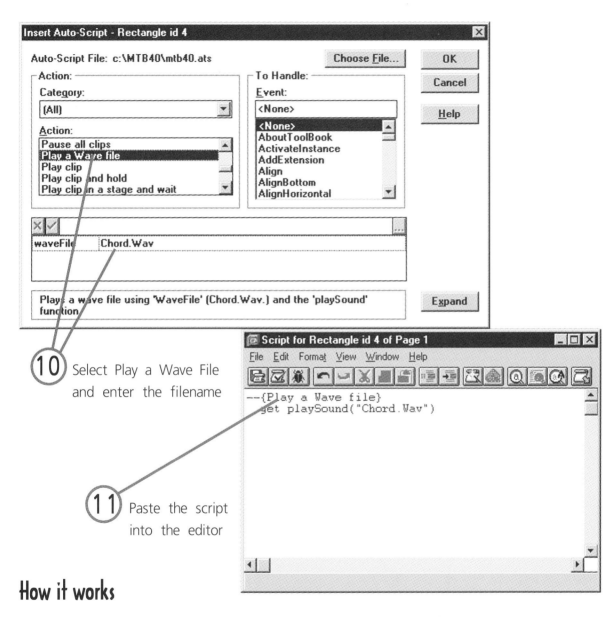

10 Select Play a Wave File and enter the filename

11 Paste the script into the editor

How it works

The square drawn over the 10 o'clock number on the image is invisible to the user, but just a normal object to Toolbook. If a user clicks on the square, Toolbook will play any script commands that are attached to the object. The user cannot see anything, since the square is transparent. Toolbook knows the square is there and will react to a mouse click. This trick is often used to create an area of an image that reacts to a mouse click.

Summary

❑ You can include **images, sound or video clips** in almost any Windows application to add sparkle to a document.

❑ Once you have embedded sound or video in a document, **any other user can see the video** or listen to the sound.

❑ Use the **macro language** of your wordprocessor to create separate pages and move between them.

❑ Presentations look professional if you use **presentation software** and stick to simple rules.

❑ **Authoring packages** allow you to develop your own multimedia title with little programming.

❑ **Script-based** authoring is flexible and powerful, but can be difficult for non-programmers.

❑ **Icon-based** authoring is simple, but can lack flexibility.

❑ **Stage-based** systems, such as Director, are easy for designers to use and understand.

❑ Creating a worthwile multimedia title takes time and requires plenty of planning beforehand.

10 Tuning Windows

Tuning for multimedia

Multimedia is very demanding on all the elements in your PC – both hardware and software. A short video clip can take several megabytes of disk space, and sound and images can soon fill up your hard disk. When you start to edit images or manipulate them with presentation software or an authoring package, you'll find that your PC is pushed to its limits.

Over the next few pages, you'll see how to tune Windows so that multimedia applications run faster and more smoothly.

Before you start to set up your PC to its optimum configuration, gather together the basic information about what it has installed: the size of hard disk, amount of RAM, video display, speed of the CD-ROM drive and so on.

Basic steps

❑ To check disk space

1 Run **Windows Explorer** or **My Computer**.

2 Click on the **C: drive** icon for your hard disk.

3 The **Free space** is displayed on the right of the Status Bar. In My Computer, you can also see the **Capacity** of the disk.

Take note

If you want to know how to check the amount of RAM memory, turn to page 22.

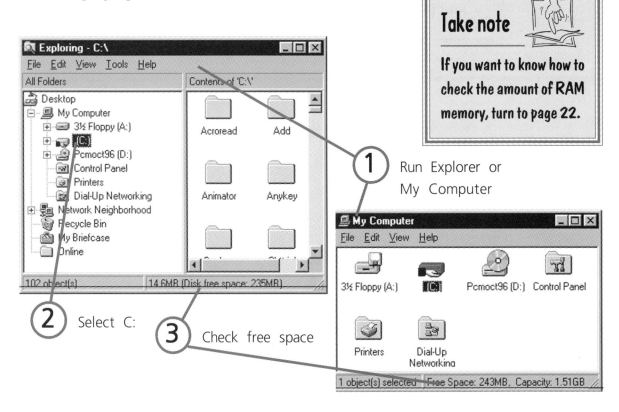

① Run Explorer or My Computer

② Select C:

③ Check free space

134

Basic steps

❏ To check your screen resolution

1 From the **Start** menu, select **Settings** then **Control Panel.**

2 Double-click on the **Display** icon.

3 Open the **Settings** tab. The screen resolution is shown in the **Desktop** area.

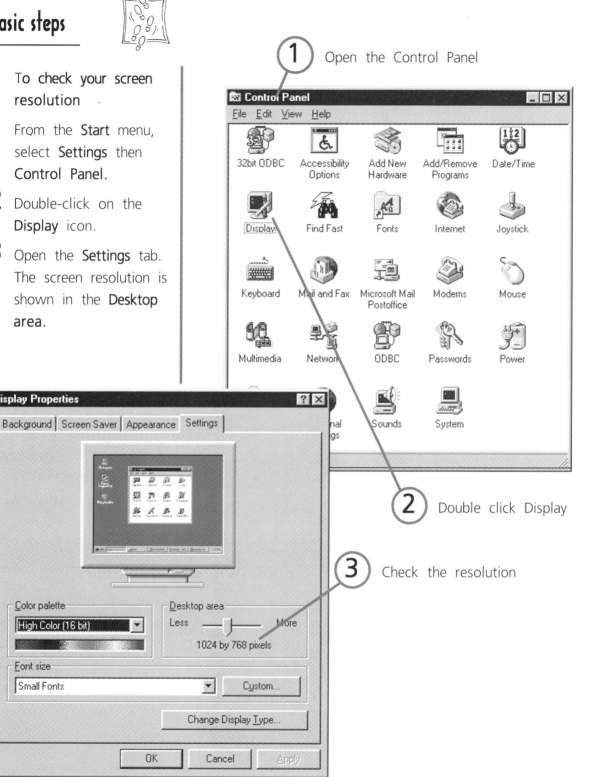

① Open the Control Panel

② Double click Display

③ Check the resolution

Performance tuning

Windows 95 includes a number of features that let you tune up your PC to work more efficiently with multimedia applications.

You can set up the CD-ROM and hard drive to read data faster, and can configure the sound card and graphics to record and display clearer sound and images.

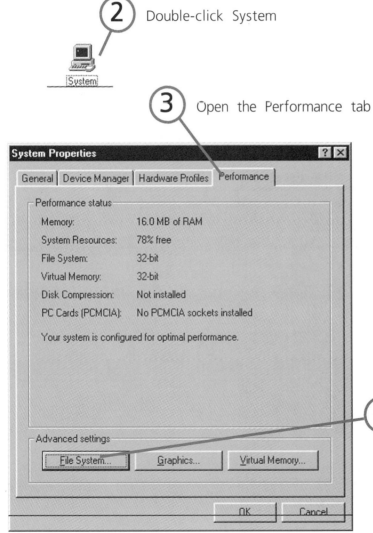

② Double-click System

System

③ Open the Performance tab

System Properties [?] [X]

| General | Device Manager | Hardware Profiles | Performance |

─ Performance status ──────────────
Memory: 16.0 MB of RAM
System Resources: 78% free
File System: 32-bit
Virtual Memory: 32-bit
Disk Compression: Not installed
PC Cards (PCMCIA):   No PCMCIA sockets installed

Your system is configured for optimal performance.

─ Advanced settings ──────────────
[File System...]   [Graphics...]   [Virtual Memory...]

[OK]   [Cancel]

④ Click File System

Basic steps

1 Open the **Control Panel**.

2 Double-click the **System** icon.

3 Switch to the **Performance** tab.

4 Click on the **File System** button.

5 On the **Hard Disk** tab, check that the **Read-ahead optimization** is set to *Full*.

6 On the **CD-ROM** tab, set the **Supplemental cache size** to *Large*.

7 Check that the **access pattern** matches the speed of your CD-ROM drive.

8 Click **OK**.

136

Using chaces

If your computer has 16Mb or more of memory, then you can set up Windows to use large cache sizes. These caches are used to improve the performance of your hard disk and CD-ROM drives. The caches use part of RAM to store frequently-used data.

The Troubleshooting tab is only for experts!

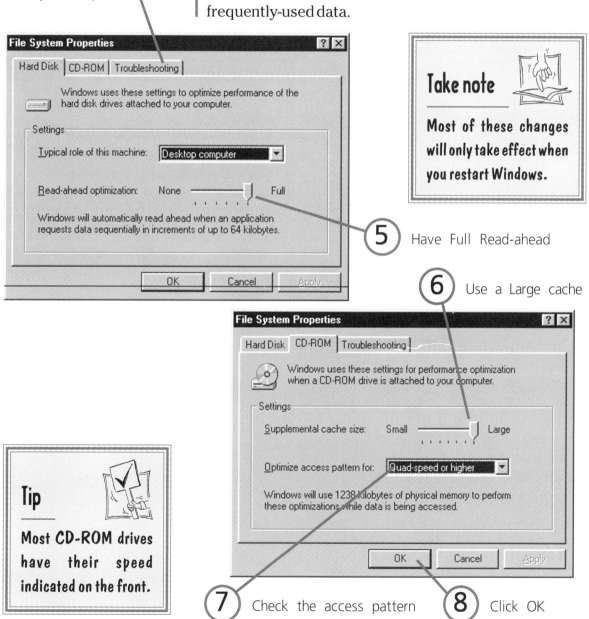

Take note

Most of these changes will only take effect when you restart Windows.

5 Have Full Read-ahead

6 Use a Large cache

Tip

Most CD-ROM drives have their speed indicated on the front.

7 Check the access pattern

8 Click OK

Summary

□ To run multimedia applications your PC needs to be set up correctly and running efficiently.

□ Set **Read-ahead optimization** to full and use **large caches** for better hard disk and CD-ROM drive performance.

Glossary

Glossary

Adapter card

Flat board with electronic components that fits into an expansion slot in your PC; used to add a feature, such as a CD-ROM controller.

Analogue signal

Signal that is continuously variable, such as speech; a PC has to convert analogue signals into numeric form before it can process them.

Analogue to digital conversion

Process of changing an analogue signal (such as a voice or music) into a stream of numbers that can then be stored on a computer. The process works by looking at the height of the analogue signal several thousand times every second and recording this as a number.

Animation

To display a sequence of drawings each slightly different to give the impression of movement.

Authoring package

Software that allows you to create your own multimedia titles by controlling images, sound, video and text on screen, and define how they react to a user's instructions.

AutoPlay

Feature of Windows 95 that will automatically run the software on a CD-ROM when it is inserted into the drive. The user doesn't have to do a thing.

AVI (Audio Video Interleaved)

Method of storing video clips with an audio signal so that it can be played back without special hardware (but it does require a video capture card to record video).

Bit (binary digit)

Smallest piece of data that a computer can handle: can either be 1 or 0; a byte is made up of eight bits.

Bitmap

Image in which the colour of each pixel is defined, rather than a vector image in which the coordinates of lines and shapes are described.

BMP

Filename extension for the standard way of storing bitmap images.

Bus

Set of parallel wires for transferring data within a PC. See also *Expansion bus*.

CD audio

Standard CD that stores music or voice.

CD Player

Utility that plays audio CDs on a multimedia PC.

CD-ROM

Flat, plastic disc that can store around 650Mb of data; the data can be video, sound, text or image data and is read using a laser beam as the disc spins.

CD-ROM XA

Standard that defines how a drive reads video and audio at the same time, also used to read PhotoCD discs.

Cel

Single image within an animation.

Channel

Method of identifying an instrument in a MIDI setup so that it receives the musical notes intended for it.

Clip art

Pre-drawn images that can be used to enhance your presentations.

Device driver

Special software that controls a piece of hardware, such as a sound card or CD-ROM drive.

Dithering

Method of giving the impression of a colour by using a pattern of different coloured pixels that the eye blends together; for example, black and white blend to give the impression of grey. Applied to curves, dithering with a lighter colour can smooth out jagged edges.

Embedding

To include a multimedia object, such as a sound file or image within another Windows application.

Expansion bus

Electrical contacts from the computer's processor that allow it to communicate with other electronic devices. For example, inside a PC are several expansion connectors that allow plug-in expansion cards to electrically connect to the computer's processor and memory.

Explorer

Utility supplied with Windows 95 that allows you to view the files stored on your disks and CD-ROMs. Also lets you delete and manage files.

FM synthesizer

One method that a sound card uses to produce sound from MIDI instructions.

Frame

A single image that is part of a series that make up a video or animation clip. Full motion video shows smooth movement by displaying around 30 separate frames every second.

Full-motion video

Video that plays back smoothly at around 30 frames every second.

Hook

Event to which a sound can be attached.

Hot link

User controlled link between one part of a multimedia title and another. May be either a *Hotspot* or a *Hot-word*.

Hotspot

Section of an image linked to a different page or event; when selecte, it moves the user to another page or activates the event.

Hot-word

Word displayed in a different colour or underlined that links to a related text, or a different page.

Hypertext

Text that contains hot-words that are linked to other sections of text; a user can click on one hot-word and this displays a related piece of text.

Interactive multimedia

Multimedia in which the user can explore the data by clicking on hotspots, buttons and hot-words.

Interlaced

Method of displaying pictures on a monitor in which the image is built up in two passes. The first pass draws in the every other line on the screen, the second pass fills in the remainder. Most monitors are interlaced.

Interrupt (IRQ)

Electrical signal generated by a sound card, disk drive, MIDI port or other device to tell the computer's processor that it wants to transfer data.

MCI (Multi Channel Interface)

Standard way of controlling multimedia devices from within Windows; MCI defines the instructions used.

Media Player

Utility (in the Accessories menu) that can play back sound, video or animation clips.

MIDI (Musical Instrument Digital Interface)

Method of linking electronic instruments and HiFi systems to, and controlling them from a PC.

Morphing software

Software which can generates an animated sequence to transform a starting image into a different end image.

MPC

Standard set of guidelines that a multimedia PC should meet.

Multisession

CD-ROM drive and controller that can read data that has been stored on the disc at two or more different times (sessions). For example, if you store some photographs on a PhotoCD, then two weeks later you store some more on the same

PhotoCD disc you have created a disc with two sessions. The second session can only be read using a multisession drive.

OLE (Object Linking and Embedding)
Windows function that lets one application use data from another; for example, to include a sound sample in a document.

Patch
Term used to describe the settings that define the sound a MIDI synthesizer will play on a particular channel.

PhotoCD
Method of storing scanned images of photographs on a CD-ROM; normally produced when your photographs are being developed and read with a CD-ROM XA drive.

Pixel (picture element)
Single dot on a screen; the smallest element that can be controlled and recoloured.

Plug and Play
Feature of Windows 95 that works on compatible PCs to simplify the job of installing new hardware. All you have to do is connect the new device and Windows will detect it and configure it automatically.

QuickTime
Method of storing video and animation clips, developed for the Macintosh but now available for PCs.

RAM (Random Access Memory)
Short term memory made of electronic chips that store data while the PC is on. They are much faster than a hard disk, but not permanent and more expensive; a modern PC normally has 16Mb.

Sampling
Process carried out by an analogue-to-digital converter (such as a sound recorder) in which the analogue signal is examined thousands of times every second and converted into numbers.

Scanner
Device that lets you turn images on paper into graphic files for use on your PC.

SCSI (Small Computer Systems Interface)
A standard for connecting devices such as a CD-ROM drive or scanner to a PC.

Sequencer
Software that works like a MIDI recorder. It stores the notes being played on a keyboard or other MIDI instrument onto a disk so that the musician can then display, edit or playback the notes.

SIMM (Single Inline Memory Module)
Small board with several memory chips mounted on it and a connector along the bottom edge. These are the usual way to expand the memory of a computer.

Sound Blaster

Probably the most popular of all the *sound cards* currently on the market, and almost a standard in itself.

Sound card

Adapter that fits into an expansion slot and connects to a speaker and microphone and lets you record sound on your hard disk and play it back through the speakers.

Sound Recorder

Utility (in the Accessories group) that lets you record, playback or edit sounds.

S-VGA (Super VGA)

Current standard for colour graphics displays that can support resolution of up to 800 x 600 pixels.

Synthesizer

Device that can generate sounds in response to data that represents musical notes. Normally, PC sound cards have a synthesizer chip that allows them to generate sounds from MIDI data. see also FM synthesizer.

Vector image

Picture that is described with lines and curves that are stored as a series of co-ordinates. This means that the quality of the image remains the same even if you zoom in on an area. Bitmap images, in comparison, store an image by defining each pixel.

VGA (Virtual Graphics Array)

Older standard for colour graphics displays that can support resolutions of up to 640 x 480 pixels.

Video clip

Real-life full-motion action stored on a PC, normally in an AVI format file.

Video RAM

Memory on a video adapter card used to store the image displayed on the monitor. If you add more memory to your video adapter you normally boost its ability to display more colours or higher resolution graphics.

WAV file

File format used to store a sound on a PC.

Wizard

Found in many applications and when installing new hardware. Wizards are screens that help you carry out complicated operations by asking you simple questions.

WordPad

Word-processing software included with Windows 95 that lets you type, edit and format documents.

Index

145